PROVENCE
quilts and cuisine

MARIE-CHRISTINE FLOCARD
COSABETH PARRIAUD

Photos by Jean-Michel André

Editor: Beate Marie Nellemann
Technical Editors: Peggy Strawhorn Kass, Lynn Koolish,
Joyce Engels Lytle, Karyn Hoyt
Copy Editors: Lucy Grijalva, Ellen Pahl
Design Direction: Aliza Kahn Shalit
Book Design and Production: Aliza Kahn Shalit
Cover Design: Aliza Kahn Shalit
Production Assistant: Stacy Chamness
Graphic Illustrations: Jeffery Carrillo

Watercolors and sketches by: Cosabeth Parriaud, page 50; Violette
Parriaud, pages 82, 109, and 112; Jean-Claude Parriaud, page 49;
Pascale Parriaud, page 21; Cécile Flocard-Shrimpton, pages 42, 64, 75,
81, 85, and 93; and Martin Tremon, pages 12, 17, 31, and 64.

Front Cover: *Fig Tree Leaves* quilt by Cosabeth Parriaud

Photography by Jean-Michel André, Barjac, 30430 France. Photos on
page 5 and 94 by Cosabeth Parriaud. Photo on page 9 by Phillipe
Bois. Photos on pages 28, 67, 76, and 89 by PhotoSpin.com.

Published by C&T Publishing, Inc.,
P.O. Box 1456 Lafayette, California 94549

Library of Congress Cataloging-in-Publication Data
Flocard, Marie-Christine,
  Provence quilts and cuisine / Marie-Christine Flocard and Cosabeth
Parriaud ; photos by Jean-Michel André.
     p. cm.
Includes index.
  ISBN 1-57120-139-4
  1. Patchwork–France–Provence–Patterns. 2. Quilting–France–Provence–
Patterns. 3. Cookery, French–Provençal style. I. Parriaud, Cosabeth,
II. Title.
  TT835 .F56 2002
  746.46'041'09449–dc21
                                        2001005175

Printed in China
10 9 8 7 6 5 4 3 2 1

Contents

To our husbands, children, families, and friends who have always appreciated our long hours with quilting and cooking.

Acknowledgments

We would like to thank all the people who helped us bring this book from dream to reality:

The C&T family for their support, especially our developmental editor, Beate Nellemann, for her enthusiasm from the very beginning, her invaluable help, her great sense of humor under any circumstance, and her friendship that helped to make the photo shoot in Provence so special.

Cosabeth's parents for their confidence, their hospitality and the keys to their family home in Provence, which for one week was our general quarters for quilting, cooking, and shooting photos.

Jean-Michel André, our friend and talented photographer, whose work and creativity have contributed immensely to this book.

Diane de Obaldia, owner of Le Rouvray in Paris, for her understanding, her encouragement, and for providing us with fabrics and supplies to make the projects for the book.

Les Olivades and staff for their kindness, for providing us with their beautiful fabrics to use in our projects, and for the elegant table accessories used in some of the photos.

Catherine l'Helgoualch, owner of La Sérénité, for her great sense of hospitality when shooting photos in her beautiful home and garden.

Cécile Flocard-Shrimpton, Martin Tremon, and the Parriaud family for their watercolors, drawings, and sketches that make this book sing.

Christine Meynier for her superb machine quilting on *Fig Tree Leaves* on page 16; Laure Paoli for her precious advice on the recipes; and Jeanne Chausson for her help with *Still Life*.

Florence and Eric Odin, Château de Potelières, Potelières (Gard); Michelle Deville, Mas d'Alzon, Vagnas (Gard); the wine shop, Les Vins de Nos Régions, Barjac (Gard); and Jean-Michel André and Françoise Favède who all let us use their homes and gardens for shooting photos.

Emmanuel Signoret, stone cutter, for making the beautiful window shown on pages 31 and 32.

And certainly not least: all our students for their encouragement.

Introduction

Provence, in southern France, with its light and spectacular landscape, has been an inspiration to artists for centuries. In 1888 Vincent van Gogh wrote in a letter to Paul Gauguin: "These days I feel an urge to work: I am occupied by a landscape: a blue sky raised above a wine field of green, purple and yellow..."

The landscape of Provence creates a unique feeling of well-being and inspiration. It is a lovely combination of culture, history, and landscape. Here you are—on the one hand very close to nature, and yet never very far from charming villages with charismatic old houses on curved streets, plazas, and promenades shaded by plane trees, where old fountains overflow with history. The inviting food markets intoxicate you with colors and a wide selection of fresh and tasty products that simultaneously stimulate and soothe. In the villages you find cafés and charming restaurants that serve local wines and food, where the townspeople meet for a leisurely chat.

It is our hope with this book on Provence to stimulate your senses, to inspire you with the richness of the landscape, and to give you a taste of the simplicity of the wonderful cuisine of Provence. The recipes presented in our book are easy to prepare, utilizing ingredients you can find all over the world.

The flavor and the ambience of Provence have inspired us to make traditional quilts: *Double Wedding Ring, Vanne Provençale, Boutis, Fig Tree Leaves,* and *Place Mats with Peaches,* as well as more contemporary ones: *Roofs of Avignon, Still Life, Memories of Provence,* and a very handy *Tote Bag.* We used French Provençal fabrics along with Provençal-style textiles, and many other fabrics that you can buy in the U.S. and other places around the world.

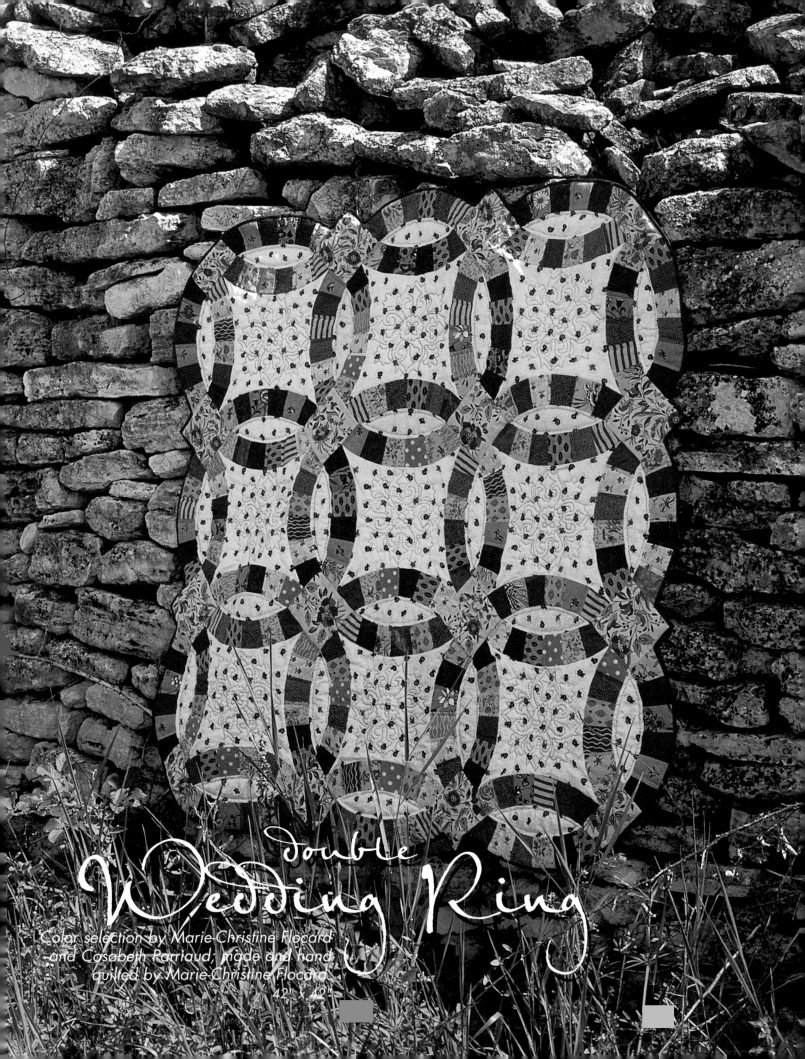

double
Wedding Ring

Color selection by Marie-Christine Flocard
and Cosabeth Parriaud; made and hand
quilted by Marie-Christine Flocard.
42" x 42"

 e have given a touch of Provençal warmth and light to this traditional American design. The colors suggest the fruits, vegetables, and flowers you find in an open-air market. The quilting pattern was inspired by the tile floor in the entry of an old Provençal home.

FABRIC SELECTION

We used a mix of American and Provençal prints.

FABRICS

1⅝ yards of light print for A and B pieces

¼ yard each of twelve different fabrics in varying shades of orange, yellow, and pink for C, Cr, and D pieces

⅓ yard of contrasting yellow print (or ¼ yard each of two different fabrics) for E pieces

1¼ yards of 55"-wide or 2⅝ yards of 42"-wide cotton fabric for backing

⅔ yard of fabric for bias binding

47" x 47" square of thin cotton batting

Other Materials

Template material

CUTTING

Template patterns are on pages 102–103. ¼" **seam allowances are included.**

1. Trace patterns A–E onto template material. Cut out the templates and transfer all markings.

2. Cut 9 A pieces from the light print using template A.

3. Cut 24 B pieces from the light print using template B.

4. Cut 48 C pieces, flip template C over to cut 48 Cr pieces, and cut 192 D pieces from the various orange, yellow, and pink prints using templates C and D. Remember to mark a notch on the shortest straight side of the C and Cr pieces.

5. Cut 48 E pieces (total) from the yellow prints using template E.

6. Cut the binding fabric to make 5¾ yards of continuous bias binding, following General Instructions, page 100.

tip

Our instructions provide a simpler method. To make a quilt exactly like the one in the photo on page 15, with squares pointing out at the edges, you can either a) cut eight additional E pieces and sew them to the side edges of the quilt or b) create a template that combines four E pieces into one larger square—note that you will still need to use pairs of E pieces in each corner of the quilt.

CONSTRUCTION
The Arcs

1. Sew four D pieces to create an arc. Add one C piece and one Cr piece to opposite ends of the arc as shown. Make sure the notched edge is sewn to the D pieces. Press seams in one direction. Make a total of forty-eight arcs.

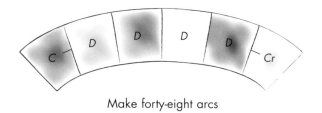

Make forty-eight arcs

Pont du Gard, one of the wonders of the Roman period, is an aqueduct that brought spring water to the city of Nîmes. It was built circa 19 B.C.

2. Add an E piece to opposite ends of twenty-four arcs from Step 1. Set the remaining twenty-four arcs aside.

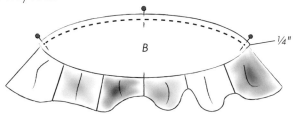

Make twenty-four

Arc/Melon Units

1. Be sure to match midpoints, and work with the B piece on top. With right-sides together, sew a short arc to one side of each B piece. Start and stop your seam ¼" from each end and backstitch. Press toward the arc. Make twenty-four.

To get perfect corners it is very important to sew only to the point where the pin goes in, at the dots on piece B (¼" from edge).

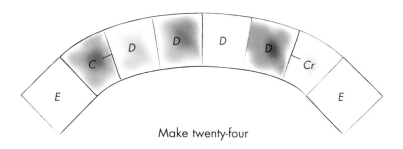

Pin and sew one short arc to the melon

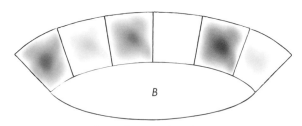

Partially completed unit

12

2. Sew a longer arc (with E pieces attached) to the other side of each unit from Step 1. Press. Make twenty-four arc/melon units.

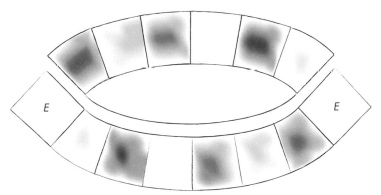

Complete the arc/melon unit

QUILT ASSEMBLY

1. With right sides together, match and pin an arc/melon unit to one side of each A piece.

Sew the units with the A piece on top. Start and stop your seam ¼" from each end, and backstitch. Make nine and set four aside.

2. Sew an arc/melon unit to remaining sides of five units from Step 1. Refer to *Double Wedding Ring* layout on this page.

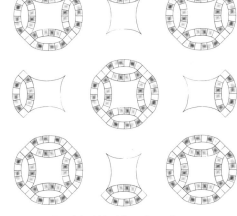

Double Wedding Ring layout

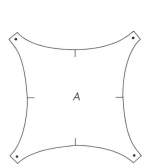

Marked A piece

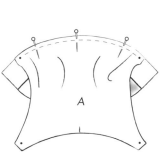

Pin and sew an arc/melon unit to each A piece

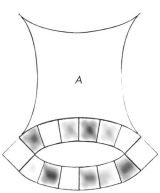

Completed unit with one arc/melon unit attached

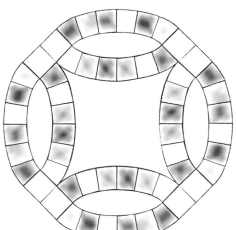

Completed unit with four arc/melon units attached

3. Sew the completed units into rows. Press seam allowances toward the arcs. Sew the rows together. Press.

QUILTING

1. Press the top flat. Trim the corner E pieces to follow the curve of the arcs.

2. Enlarge and trace the quilting design below to fill the A pieces on the quilt top. We adapted the design from an old Provençal tile, but you can use any design that fits the space. Look around for inspiration.

3. Layer and baste the quilt, see pages 98–99. Quilt as preferred by hand or machine.

4. Trim batting and backing even with the quilt top. Bind using the continuous bias binding made earlier.

Detail of quilting design

Quilting design; enlarge 130% to 6" x 6"

Below, from left to right:
Double Wedding Ring;
detail of a tile floor in an
old Provençal house;
Double Wedding Ring

14

Double Wedding Ring, 42" x 42"

Fig Tree Leaves

Designed and appliquéd by Cosabeth Parriaud;
machine quilted by Christine Meynier.
54½" x 54½"

ig trees grow all over Provence, where they are considered a symbol of abundance. Elegant branches hold the large, serrated leaves that inspired us to design this quilt. The fruit ranges in color from green to purple, according to the variety, and may be eaten raw, dried, in desserts, or cooked in marmalade or gratin. It is especially delicious to eat the ripe figs when they have just been picked from the trees in the garden at the end of the summer.

FABRIC SELECTION

To obtain a rich palette, we chose several greens that are analogous on the color wheel (pure green, yellow-green, and blue-green) and varied in value and intensity. We painted the leaves and fruit with textile paint to give them a more natural look.

FABRICS

2¼ yards of off-white fabric for background squares

1 yard total of assorted green fabrics for leaves. We used six.

¼ yard total of assorted purple fabrics for figs. We used three.

Scraps of brown for stems

1¾ yards of green fabric for the border

3½ yards of cotton fabric for backing

½ yard purple fabric for binding

59" x 59" square of thin cotton batting

Other Materials

Template material

Textile paints in red, yellow, blue, black, and white. Use paints that you can dilute with water, and can be heat-set with an iron. See Sources, page 110.

Paintbrushes

Capitelles (also called Bories)

These curious-looking dry stone huts—made with slabs called Lauzes—date back to the Iron Age. They were built all over Provence until the eighteenth century for use as tool sheds and sheep pens.

When tracing, reverse the templates once in a while to add more interest to the design.

CUTTING

1. Cut five 14½" x 42"-wide strips from the off-white fabric. Cut into nine squares, each 14½" x 14½".

2. Cut four 6½" x 60" strips of green fabric lengthwise.

3. Cut six 2" x 42"-wide strips of purple fabric.

Appliqué Pieces

Appliqué patterns are on page 103. **Turn-under allowances are not included.** Read about Appliqué Techniques (pages 94–96) to select your preferred appliqué method.

4. Use a photocopy machine to enlarge patterns 200%. Trace them onto template material. Cut out the templates.

Leaves

5. Cut five leaves from the assorted green fabrics using template A.

6. Cut four leaves from the assorted green fabrics using template B.

Figs

7. Cut five figs from the assorted purple fabrics using template C.

8. Cut four figs from the assorted purple fabrics using template D.

Stems

9. Cut nine stems from the different brown scraps using template E.

CONSTRUCTION

For guidance in painting the leaves, the figs, and the stems, see Fabric Painting, page 96.

Add veins, irregular dots, and stains here and there on the leaves. We also added touches of white on the figs, touches of red on the stems, and other highlights.

Be imaginative and use different colors and shapes. Do not try to be too realistic.

Follow the instructions on the paint labels carefully.

1. Prepare the paints, mixing colors to your satisfaction.

2. Paint the figs, leaves, and stems before appliquéing them to the background fabric. Heat set the paints as directed by the paint manufacturer.

3. Refer to the diagram below to position and appliqué the leaves and stems to the 14½" blocks. Note that the leaf hides the end of the stem.

QUILT ASSEMBLY

1. Refer to the *Fig Tree Leaves* layout on this page and arrange the nine blocks, alternating colors and directions of leaves. Sew the blocks into rows. Press seams open.

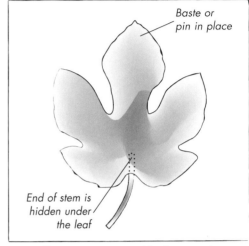

Baste or pin in place

End of stem is hidden under the leaf

Position a stem and leaf on each background block

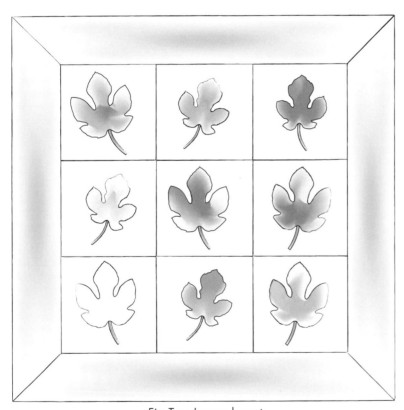

Fig Tree Leaves layout

2. Join the rows, making sure to match the seams between the blocks.

3. Piece and add the green border strips as directed in Borders with Mitered Corners, page 97.

4. Arrange the figs, referring to the photo of the quilt, page 22.

5. Appliqué them with a matching thread. To add variety we shortened some of the stalks.

QUILTING

1. Press the top flat. Layer and baste the quilt, see page 99. Quilt as preferred by hand or machine or follow our quilting suggestions below.

Quilting the Blocks

2. Start from one edge in the seam between two blocks. Quilt until you reach the leaf, quilt along the leaf for about 1¾", and then turn back until you reach the same block edge. Quilt in the seam for about 1¾" and repeat. Do this on the entire block. Change directions of the quilting lines from one block to another.

Stitch continuously without breaking the thread. After you have quilted the inside of the block, quilt around the leaf and fig in an unbroken line.

Detail of quilting

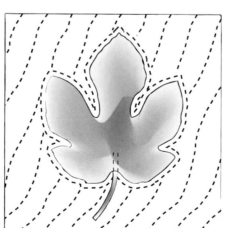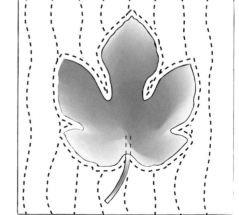

Quilting suggestions for blocks

Detail of fig

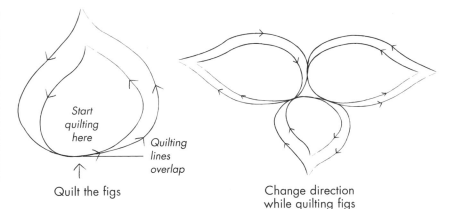
Quilting the Purple Dots

We added small purple dots on the background of the blocks for more texture and color.

3. Use the same thread in the bobbin and on the spool. Make tiny stitches, turning tight circles. Do not cut the thread but jump to another circle, and continue. Cut the connecting threads when you have stitched the final dot.

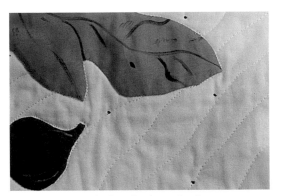

Detail of quilted purple dots

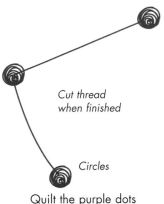

Cut thread when finished

Circles

Quilt the purple dots

After quilting each set of figs, you will need to jump to start another set. Cut the connecting threads when you have finished all of the figs.

Quilting the Border

The border is quilted with the design of figs. We recommend you practice on a small piece of fabric basted with batting and backing to get used to the motif before starting the whole border.

4. Start quilting from the stalk or the bottom of a fig (not from a side). Take care to overlap the quilting lines at the bottom of the motif, and to change the direction of the fig each time.

Detail of quilted border

Start quilting here

Quilting lines overlap

Quilt the figs

Change direction while quilting figs

Trim batting and backing even with the quilt top. Sew the purple binding following the directions on page 99.

Fig Tree Leaves, 54½" x 54½"

Boutis Provençal

Designed by Renée Gosse;
made by Marie-Christine Flocard.
18½" x 18½"

Examples of boutis: a bib,
a needle case, a purse,
and Christmas ornament.
All made by Renée Gosse.

B outis is an ancient Sicilian technique, introduced into southern France in the sixteenth century. The name comes from the Provençal word *bourrer* which means "to stuff." The name is also used for the long flexible needle used for stuffing.

Traditionally, Provençal women made wedding petticoats, baby bonnets, bibs, and counterpanes with elaborate hand stitching to celebrate the main events in life. Today in France boutis is back in fashion, and even in our busy society many women allow themselves hours to spend on this old charming method. The technique is similar to trapunto although the boutis is totally reversible; the design appears the same on both sides.

The design for the project boutis was created by Renée Gosse, and given to Marie-Christine, who made the boutis for her daughter Cécile's birthday.

FABRICS

¾ yard of white 100% cotton fabric for the top and backing. **Do not prewash.**

¼ yard of white fabric for binding (optional)

Other Materials

Fine white cotton cording or yarn—approximately 30 yards of 1⁄16" (2 mm) or 1⁄8" (4 mm) cording or 6 oz of 100% good quality cotton yarn

Approximately 1 yard cotton (or any thin) batting for stuffing, cut into 3⁄16" x 10" strips

A number 18 blunt-end tapestry needle and a trapunto needle

Quilting or embroidery hoop

Fine wooden orange stick

Ruler and a #2 pencil

100% white cotton thread for stitching

Hand quilting needle

Tracing paper and a fine-point black felt pen

Materials used for boutis

CUTTING

Cut two 20½" x 20½" squares of the white cotton.

Optional. Cut three 1¼" x 42" strips from the white fabric for binding. See Finishing, page 27.

CONSTRUCTION

Central motif pattern is on page 104.

1. Carefully press the two white fabric squares.

2. Enlarge the central motif pattern 250% on a photocopy machine. Transfer the enlarged pattern to tracing paper with a fine-point black felt pen.

3. With a sharp pencil lightly mark the center (O) of one of the two square pieces of fabric.

4. Mark the two medians and the diagonals. Draw a line around the perimeter of the square, ½" from the edge. Add three additional border lines ³⁄₁₆" apart.

5. Place the tracing paper pattern under the fabric, matching the center and all other markings. Pin. With the pencil, lightly trace the entire design.

6. Choose any quadrant of the design and make a point midway along its diagonal line. Using a ruler for accuracy, draw one line across this quarter of the quilt; repeat every ³⁄₁₆" to fill the quadrant. Do the same in the remaining three quadrants. These lines, when stitched, form the channels through which you will pull the cording.

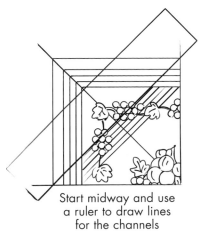

Start midway and use a ruler to draw lines for the channels

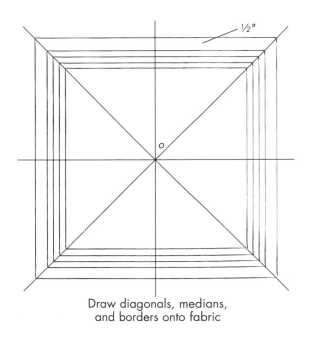

Draw diagonals, medians, and borders onto fabric

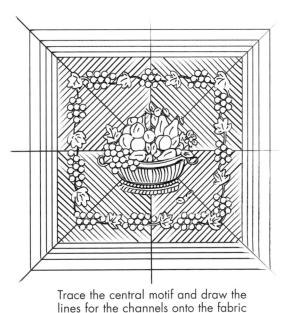

Trace the central motif and draw the lines for the channels onto the fabric

When stuffing a leaf, petal, or fruit, work from the edge of the motif and not from the center. The tiny holes you create inserting the stuffing are more likely to disappear when you wash the boutis.

QUILT ASSEMBLY

1. Place the marked fabric on top of the backing fabric, wrong sides together. Smooth any wrinkles. Baste with long stitches.

2. Place the basted work loosely in a quilting or embroidery hoop.

3. Starting in the center, follow the traced lines to stitch the two layers together with small running stitches, as you do for quilting. Complete the design motifs in the center and around the outer edge before starting to stitch the diagonal channel lines. Hide the knots between the two layers of fabric.

4. Remove the work from the hoop.

Stuffing

5. Use the ³⁄₁₆" x 10" batting strips to begin stuffing the central motif. Work from the back, starting with the fruit. Work toward the basket using a needle and a fine orange stick to maneuver the stuffing as follows:

a. With the needle, separate the threads of the backing fabric without breaking them. Do not cut the fabric. With the orange stick gently push the strips of batting into the opening to stuff the motif. Be patient; this process takes time. Do not over-stuff. The quilt should remain supple.

b. Close the holes as you go by moving the threads back into place with a sharp needle. Finish all stuffing before you begin cording. Do not worry if you still have some tiny holes; they will disappear when you wash the finished boutis.

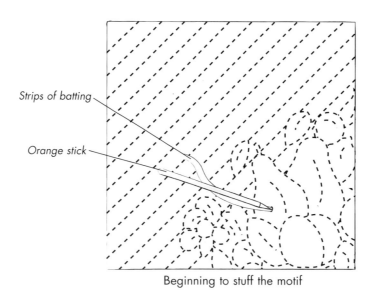

Strips of batting

Orange stick

Beginning to stuff the motif

Cording

1. Thread a trapunto or tapestry needle with the cotton cording or yarn. The length of the cording/yarn will depend on the length of the channel. Based on the width, we used one to two strands in the narrow channels and three to four strands in the other channels. Do **not** knot the cording/yarn.

2. Working from the back, insert the needle through the fabric in each stitched channel, and gently pull the cording/yarn. On the diagonal channels, work from the corners toward the center. You will go from one edge to the other on the diagonal.

3. Pull the needle out on the same side of the work as you entered. Clip the yarn close to the needle exit point, and use the tip of needle to poke the end of the cording/yarn back into the hole. Close the opening as you did when you completed the stuffing. Each time the channel reaches the vine or the central motif, you will need to exit and restart

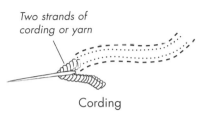

Two strands of cording or yarn

Cording

A few potters in Anduze, a city in the Cévennes area, still duplicate this traditional sixteenth century vase. The traditional colors are a combination of green, honey, and auburn glaze, but they are also made in only green-blue or honey. The vase is easily recognized by its wreath and three stamped emblems. See Sources, page 110, for more information.

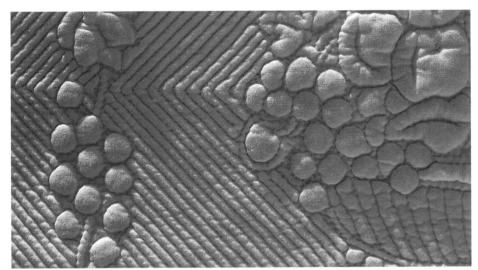

Detail of the boutis

FINISHING

1. Cut the back fabric only, 3/16" from the last stitched line. Double fold the front fabric over to the back and blindstitch on the back along the last stitched line. If you prefer, finish the work with a narrow binding made from the white fabric. Refer to Binding directions on page 99.

2. Wash your finished boutis in cold to lukewarm water with a neutral, pH-balanced soap. Rinse well, roll in a towel, and squeeze out excess moisture. Dry flat. Never iron.

Memories of Provence

Designed, made, and machine quilted by Cosabeth Parriaud.
26½" x 42½"

P R O V E N C E

FABRIC SELECTION

Transferring photos onto fabric is a lot of fun, and is a great way to remember your favorite places and people. We combined transferred photos with traditional Provençal fabrics printed by the French company Les Olivades (see Sources, page 110).

FABRICS

We suggest selecting various values and intensities of each color.

4 fat quarters (18" x 22") of blue fabrics

3 fat quarters (18" x 22") of green fabrics

3 fat quarters (18" x 22") of red fabrics

3 fat quarters (18" x 22") of yellow fabrics

1 fat quarter (18" x 22") of cream fabric

1 yard white, smoothly woven cotton (200 count is best), for photo transfer

1½ yards of cotton fabric for backing

⅓ yard of red fabric for binding

31" x 47" piece of thin cotton batting

Other Materials

Smoky monofilament thread

Eight photos, each 4" x 6". We used two horizontal and six vertical photos.

Photo transfer paper (See Sources, page 110)

An iron, preferably without steam holes

Cut sixteen half-square triangles each for B and C, and twelve each for E and F

CUTTING

Refer to the photo on page 34, note how the pieces are cut from the different fabrics.

1. Cut four 3½" x 3½" squares, each from a different color for A.

2. Cut two 3" x 3" squares, each from four different colors.
Cut them once on the diagonal to make sixteen half-square B triangles.

3. Cut two 3⅞" x 3⅞" squares, each of four different colors.
Cut them once on the diagonal to make sixteen half-square C triangles.

4. Cut three 4½" x 4½" squares, each from a different color for D.

5. Cut two 3¾" x 3¾" squares, each from three different colors.
Cut them once on the diagonal to make twelve half-square E triangles.

6. Cut two 4⅞" x 4⅞" squares, each from three different colors.
Cut them once on the diagonal to make twelve half-square F triangles.

7. Cut four additional 3½" x 3½" A squares for borders.

8. Cut eight 3½" x 6½" G rectangles for borders.

9. Cut eight 3½" x 8½" H rectangles for borders.

10. Cut eight 8½" x 12" rectangles from white fabric for the photo transfer blocks.

11. Cut four 2" x 42" strips of green fabric for binding.

TRANSFERRING PHOTOS

We recommend testing the transfer process on an extra piece of fabric before transferring your final photos. The secret is in the heat of the iron and the pressure.

For more information on photo transfer materials and services see Sources, page 110.

If you find it difficult to do yourself, take your photos and transfer paper to a copy shop that offers transfer services.

1. Enlarge the photos 170% (to 6½" x 10") on a photocopy machine and photocopy the enlarged photos onto photo transfer sheets, using the mirror-image option. Or you may scan your photos into a computer and enlarge them to 6½" x 10", then use a bubble jet or color laser printer to print the photos on the transfer sheets.

2. Follow the manufacturer's directions to transfer the photo images to the eight pieces of white cotton.

Photo Blocks

Cut transferred photos into 6½" x 8½" rectangles.

The Camargue cross features a heart and an anchor, surmounted by a Roman cross. On the upper extremities are the guardian's three-pronged stick; the lower one features a heart. This cross embodies the three evangelical virtues: faith (the cross), hope (the anchor), and charity (the heart).

Memories of Provence

CONSTRUCTION
Block One

1. Sew a B triangle to each side of an A square.
Press seams toward triangles.

2. Sew a C triangle to each side of the A/B unit. Press seams toward triangles. Repeat to make four blocks. Square block to 6½" x 6½", and trim the triangle "ears."

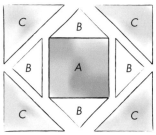 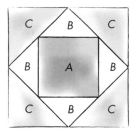

Make four of Block One

Block Two

1. Sew an E triangle to each side of a D square. Press seams toward triangles.

2. Sew an F triangle to each side of the D/E unit. Press seams toward triangles. Repeat to make three blocks. Square block to 8½" x 8½", and trim the triangle "ears."

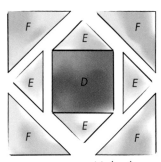 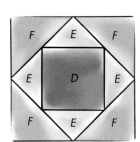

Make three of Block Two

QUILT ASSEMBLY

1. Refer to the *Memories of Provence* layout on the next page. Arrange the pieced blocks, photo blocks, squares, and border pieces into seven rows.

2. Sew blocks together into rows. Press seams away from the pieced blocks.

3. Sew the rows together.

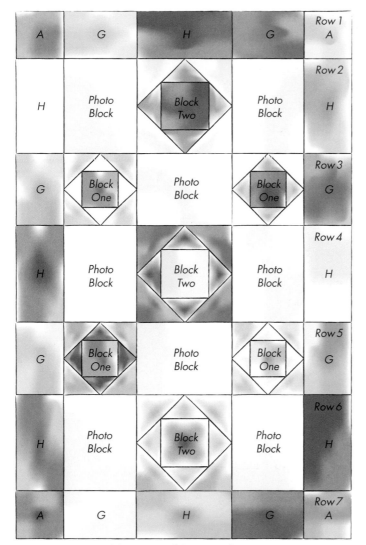

		Row 1		
A	G	H	G	A

				Row 2
H	Photo Block	Block Two	Photo Block	H

				Row 3
G	Block One	Photo Block	Block One	G

				Row 4
H	Photo Block	Block Two	Photo Block	H

				Row 5
G	Block One	Photo Block	Block One	G

				Row 6
H	Photo Block	Block Two	Photo Block	H

		Row 7		
A	G	H	G	A

Memories of Provence layout

tip

If you press the transfers be careful when you use your iron. Some brands smear from the heat. Place a piece of fabric or a Teflon™ pressing sheet on the ironing board and another one on top of the quilt to prevent the photo transfers from sticking.

QUILTING

1. Press the top flat. Layer the quilt top and baste, see page 99. Quilt as preferred, or follow our quilting suggestions. We machine quilted this project, using smoky monofilament thread.

Pictures: We outlined the major lines of the photos, adding more lines as necessary.

Pieced Blocks: We followed the diagonals and medians of each block.

Border: We quilted the diagonals of both the squares and the rectangles in the border.

2. Trim batting and backing even with the quilt top. Sew the binding following the directions on page 99.

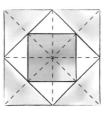

Quilting suggestions for the pieced blocks and border

33

Memories of Provence, 26½" x 42½"

34

Vanne Provençale

Designed, pieced, and hand quilted by Marie-Christine Flocard.
87" x 87"

The original, mainly floral designs for toiles de Jouy were multicolored and printed with wooden blocks. Printing with copper plates made it possible to have the single-color designs on light backgrounds that are common today.

I n Provence, a vanne is a quilted bedcover. It can be a wholecloth quilt or, as in this project, a center of solid color and borders made from other fabric such as printed toiles de Jouy or Provençal fabrics. See Sources, page 110. This vanne was made using a toile fabric, for the wedding of Marie-Christine's daughter Cécile.

FABRIC SELECTION

Marie-Christine has extensive knowledge of these toile fabrics. She lives near Jouy en Josas, the village where the fabrics were printed in the eighteenth and nineteenth centuries. The design of the toile used in this quilt dates from 1790, and is still printed today under the name "Indus" by Frey-Braquenié.

FABRICS

Note: Measurements are based on fabrics of various widths as indicated.

2⅜ yards of 60"-wide off-white fabric for the center square and middle border

4 yards of 55"-wide or 5 yards of 42"-wide toile or printed fabric for the inner and outer borders

8¼ yards of 42"-wide fabric for backing and binding

92" x 92" square of thin cotton batting

CUTTING
From the 60"-Wide Off-White Fabric

1. Cut one 52½" x 52½" square for the Center.

2. Cut five 2½" x 60" strips for the middle border.

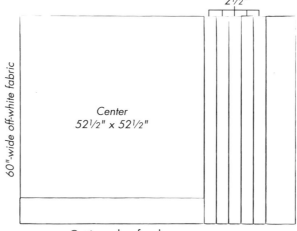

Cutting plan for the center square and the middle border

55"-Wide Toile or Printed Fabric

3. Cut five strips 55" x 2½" for the inner border.

4. Cut eight strips 55" x 14" for the outer border.

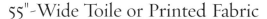

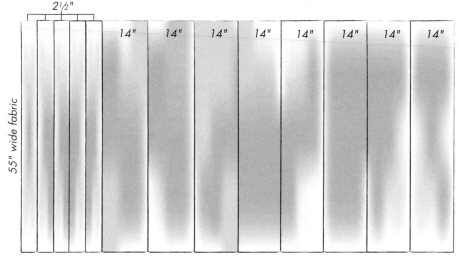

Cutting plan for the inner and outer borders from 55"-wide fabric

42"-Wide Printed Fabric

5. Cut two strips 2½" x 180" for the inner border.

6. Cut four strips 14" x 90" for the outer border.

Cutting plan for the inner and outer borders from 42"-wide fabric

42"-Wide Backing Fabric

7. Cut one 42" x 95" piece for the backing.

8. Cut two 25" x 95" pieces for the backing.

9. Cut four 2½" x 95" strips from leftover lengths for binding.

Since the religious wars in the seventeenth century between Catholics and Protestants, this cross has been the symbol of the Huguenots. Many of them were living in the south part of France. This cross features the Maltese cross from which the Languedoc cross is derived. The dove represents the Holy Spirit.

Huguenot cross made
from wrought iron

Add the inner and middle borders

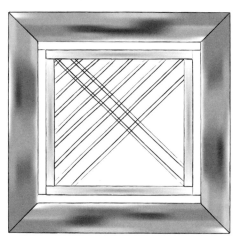

Mark the quilting lines
in the center square

QUILT ASSEMBLY

1. Piece and add the 2½"-wide toile or printed border strips as directed in Borders with Straight Corners, page 97.

2. Repeat to piece and add the 2½"-wide off-white middle border.

3. Piece and add the 14"-wide toile or printed outer border strips as directed in Borders with Mitered Corners, pages 97–98.

QUILTING

Quilting patterns are on page 105.

1. Press the quilt top flat. Use a pencil and ruler to lightly mark one diagonal line from corner to corner in the center square of the quilt top. Mark a second line ¼" to the left of this diagonal. Mark this double line every 2" all the way to one corner, and then to the opposite corner.

2. Repeat Step 1 to mark the opposite diagonals to complete a 2" grid.

3. Use the quilting patterns to mark the inner and middle borders. Start marking in the center, and work to the corners, reversing direction at the midpoint.

4. Beginning at the center, mark each outer border with double ¼" lines 3" apart. Use a ruler with a 45° marking to be sure you maintain a consistent angle.

5. Layer and baste the quilt top, see page 99.

6. Quilt using off-white quilting thread for the center square and middle borders. Use a matching thread for the toile or printed borders.

7. Trim batting and backing even with the quilt top. Sew the binding following the directions on page 99. Because of the weight of the quilt we used a wider double binding (2½" instead of 2").

Mark the quilting lines for the outer border

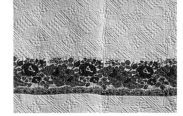

Detail of quilt pattern in second border   Detail of quilting pattern in the Center

If you prefer making a smaller project, a tablecloth is a good idea. Our friend, Annick Huet made this beautiful tablecloth using white fabric and a typical Provençal print.

Tablecloth, 57" x 57", made by Annick Huet

Since the seventeenth century, Provence has developed a strong textile tradition. It began with import of cotton toiles from India called Indiennes, and continued with the creation of manufactures (textile mills) which printed floral calicos and other colorful motifs called painted toiles. The toiles were first printed with wooden blocks, and then with copper plates. The first written evidence of this new industry appears in Marseille and dates from 1648.

Still Life

Designed, made, and machine quilted by Cosabeth Parriaud.

32½" x 40½"

his quilt reflects our love for quilting and for cooking! Many of the appliqué pieces represent ingredients used in our recipes. It may look complicated, but this quilt is not difficult at all to make. The background is made of squares and rectangles; the appliqué pieces are fused in place and then machine quilted.

FABRIC SELECTION

Choose solids, tone-on-tone solids, or marbleized fabrics for the background. The same kind of fabrics will also work for the appliqué pieces, but you can use prints as well. Dig into your scrap bag for the small pieces such as the garlic heads, tomatoes, and so on.

FABRICS
Background

½ yard of blue 1 fabric

1 fat quarter (18" x 22") of black tone-on-tone 1 fabric

1 fat quarter (18" x 22") of black tone-on-tone 2 fabric

6" x 17" piece of black tone-on-tone 3 fabric

⅛ yard of solid black fabric

5" x 9" piece of blue 2 fabric

9" x 11" piece of blue-green 1 fabric

6" x 10" piece of blue-green 2 fabric

9" x 12" piece of light blue-gray fabric

10" x 14" piece of gray fabric

9" x 11" piece of brown 1 fabric

6" x 11" piece of brown 2 fabric

10" x 11" piece of brown 3 fabric

1½ yards of cotton fabric for backing

⅓ yard of burgundy fabric for binding

36" x 44" piece of thin cotton batting

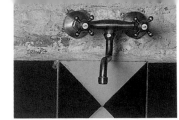

Appliqué

Scraps of reds, greens, yellow-greens, blue-greens, tans, grays, and red-purples. You will need a minimum length of:

16" of tan fabric for the baguette
16" of medium-dark yellow-green fabric for Bottle A
18" of blue-green for Bottle B

Other Materials

Template material

Textile paints (optional)

Fusible web

Smoky monofilament thread

tip

To achieve the effect of transparency in the bottles: for piece C, choose a fabric darker in value than the fabric used in Bottle A.

CUTTING
Background

1. Cut squares and rectangles from the appropriate fabrics, referring to the *Still Life* layout on this page.

2. Cut four 2" x 42" strips from the burgundy fabric for binding.

Appliqué Pieces

Appliqué patterns are on pages 106–107. Read Machine Appliqué Using Fusible Web, page 95.

3. Enlarge the patterns A–M 133% on a photocopy machine. Trace them onto template material. Seam allowances are not needed.

4. Before cutting, mark each template to indicate the right side. Cut out templates.

5. Position each template on the appropriate fabric, right side of template to wrong side of fabric and trace.

6. Cut out each shape allowing at least ¼" all around each piece. This allowance will be trimmed after the shapes are painted and the fusible web is applied.

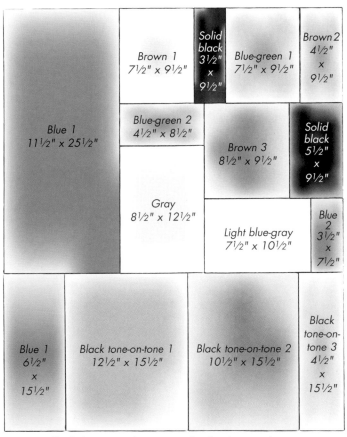

Still Life layout with cut sizes for background pieces

CONSTRUCTION
Making the Background

Referring to the Assembly diagram below, sew the squares and rectangles into units. Sew the units together to complete the background: Sew Unit 2 to Unit 3, then join to Unit 4. Add Unit 1 to the top of Unit 2–4; then join to Unit 5. Add Unit 6 to the bottom of Unit 1–5. Press all seams open.

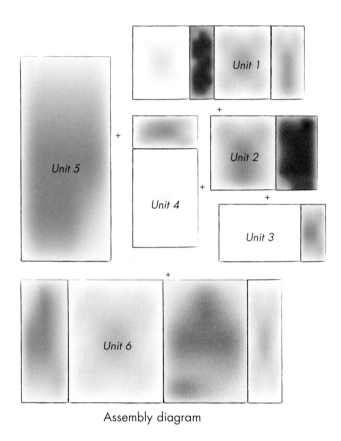

Assembly diagram

Painting the Appliqués

For guidance painting the appliqués, see Fabric Painting, page 96.

Painting the appliqué pieces is optional, but it is highly recommended on solid fabrics. We painted accents on the eggplant, zucchini, heads of garlic, baguette, olive twig, and the glass. Remember, you will re-cut the appliqué pieces to their actual size (the size of the template) just before fusing. We added brown lines to the baguette, a dark line to define the rim of the glass, touches of different greens and off-white to the zucchini, black lines and touches of dark yellow-green on the heads of garlic, and white, brown, and green touches on the olive twig. Use your imagination.

Once you have painted the pieces, let them dry, and fix the color according to the directions provided by the paint manufacturer.

PROVENCE

Detail of the
painted appliqués

Fusing the Appliqués

1. Trace the templates made earlier, wrong side up, onto the paper side of the fusible web. Cut out the shapes leaving ⅛"–¼" beyond the traced line.

2. Fuse the cut-out web to the wrong side of the appliqué fabric.
Trim to the traced line.

3. Remove the paper backing by scoring the paper lightly with a pin.

4. Position and fuse the appliqué pieces to the background in the following order, referring to the quilt photo on page 47 for placement.

a. Fuse piece C onto Bottle A, matching the edges.

b. Fuse Bottle B onto the quilt background.

c. Fuse the A/C Bottle onto the quilt background, partially covering Bottle B and matching the outer lines of the two bottles.

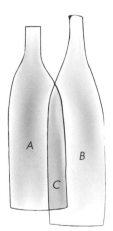

Fuse and overlap
the bottles

45

d. Position and fuse the other pieces. The olive twig is covered by one head of garlic and by the olives. Fuse the tomatoes and eggplant first, then add the leaves on the tomatoes and the narrow stalk on the eggplant.

QUILTING

1. Press the top flat. Layer and baste the quilt top, see page 99. Quilt as preferred or follow our quilting suggestions. We free-motion machine quilted this project with a smoky monofilament thread. The background was quilted with horizontal and vertical lines.

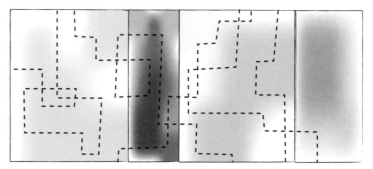

Quilting suggestion for the background

The bottles were quilted with meandering lines.

The other appliqués were quilted with curved lines that followed each shape.

Detail of painted appliqués

2. Trim batting and backing even with quilt top. Sew the binding following the directions on page 99.

Still Life, 32½" x 40½"

Roofs of Avignon

Designed by Cosabeth Parriaud;
color selection by Marie-Christine
Flocard and Cosabeth Parriaud;
made and hand quilted by
Marie-Christine Flocard.
50" x 44"

e were inspired to make this quilt while looking at a photo of the roofs of Avignon, which make beautiful puzzles of shapes and colors. Perhaps the loveliest city of Provence, Avignon stretches along the Rhône River. This city is also famous for the French children's song *Sur le Pont d'Avignon*, and for the *Palais des Papes*, the Gothic palace of the Popes that dates back to the fourteenth century.

The delicate silhouette of bell cages crown tall religious, civic, and military buildings. The cages were built to resist the local strong wind called the mistral. The mistral blows through the wrought iron instead of knocking down the bell tower itself.

FABRIC SELECTION

Most of the fabrics we used are from Cherrywood Fabrics. See Sources, page 110.

FABRICS

2½ yards total of fifty fabrics in a range of ochre, sand, brown, red, burgundy, pink, and green for pieces A–O. You can work with fewer fabrics; however, we suggest a minimum of fifteen fabrics.

2¾ yards of fabrics for backing

Leftover pieces from the top for binding

54" x 48" piece of thin cotton batting

Other Materials

Template material

Smoky monofilament thread

Three typical images in the Provençal landscape; Cypress trees, olive trees, and bell cages.

Alternate design ideas
for *Roofs of Avignon*

CUTTING

Template patterns are on pages 108–109.

All pieces are cut from assorted fabrics. Label the pieces by letter as you cut. There will be ninety-three pieces total.

1. Cut twelve 4½" x 4½" squares for A.

2. Cut five 4½" x 8½" rectangles for D.

3. Cut four 4⅞" x 4⅞" squares. Cut them once on the diagonal to make half-square E triangles. Set one aside for another project.

4. Cut one 2½" x 4½" rectangle for G.

5. Cut three 8⅞" x 8⅞" squares. Cut them once on the diagonal to make half-square H triangles.

6. Cut four 8½" x 8½" squares for I.

7. Cut two 2½" x 8½" rectangles for J.

8. Enlarge the B, C, F, and K–O patterns 200% on a photocopy machine and trace onto template material. Cut out templates.

9. Cut six B and eight B reversed, ten C, one F, five K and five K reversed, nine L, four M and two M reversed, three N, and three O.

CONSTRUCTION

1. Arrange all the pieces on a design wall referring to the *Roofs of Avignon* layout on page 51. When you are pleased with the balance of color, assemble the pieces into rows. Press each row toward one direction.

2. Sew the rows together. Press the seams open between the rows.

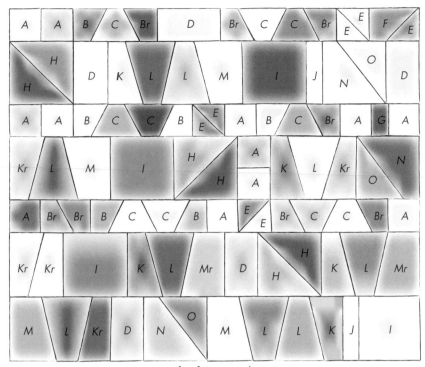

Roofs of Avignon layout

QUILTING

1. Press the quilt top flat. Use a photocopy machine to enlarge the quilting design below 200%.

2. Trace the enlarged quilting design on the quilt top with a marking tool. The motif represents the Roman tiles typical of this part of France.

3. Layer and baste the quilt top, see page 99.

Quilt as preferred by hand or machine, or follow our quilting suggestions below.

4. Trim batting and backing even with the quilt top. Piece the leftover fabric together to make a single 2" x 198" binding strip. Sew the binding following the directions on page 99.

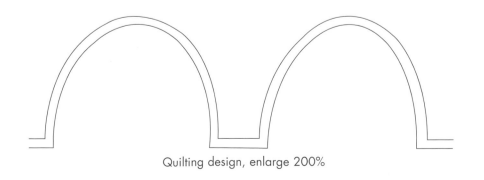

Quilting design, enlarge 200%

A *genoise*

The genoise *is a typical architectural element in Provence. It is a decorative frieze composed of a double or triple row of Roman tiles set into the wall under the eaves.*

Roofs of Avignon, 50" x 44"

Place Mats with Peaches

Designed, made, and machine
quilted by Cosabeth Parriaud.
14½" x 18½"

*P*lace mats are convenient as they can be used on any size table. Use them on your garden table for an outdoor meal, or on top of a nice matching tablecloth for a more elegant look. Finish the setting with our Peaches Cooked in Red Wine with Fresh Mint recipe (page 89).

The peaches and leaves on the place mats are fused onto the background fabric. We chose a selection of soft colors but these place mats would be nice with bright colors, too. Because you don't need much fabric for the appliqués, it may be a good occasion to use your scraps. You could even use a different fruit for each mat.

FABRIC SELECTION

We chose a combination of American, Provençal, and Dutch fabrics in soft tones. See Sources, page 110.

FABRICS (Yardage and directions are given for six place mats)

⅓ yard each of six different stripes and plaids for place mat backgrounds

Scraps of different yellows, pinks, and greens for peach and leaf appliqués. (You will need a minimum of 3" x 3" squares for the peaches. We used eight pinks and yellows for the peaches and twelve greens for the leaves.)

1½ yards total of assorted fabrics for backing

¾ yard total of fabric for binding. If you want to use different fabrics to bind each place mat, you will need ⅛ yard for each place mat.

1½ yards of Pellon® fleece or thin cotton batting

Other Materials

Template material

Fusible web

CUTTING

1. Cut pieces A–D from the various striped and plaid fabrics. Each place mat is different, but you can cut them as you wish. For the six place mats:

a. Cut twelve 7½" x 7½" squares for A.

b. Cut twelve 2½" x 14½" rectangles for B.

c. Cut six 3½" x 14½" rectangles for C.

d. Cut six 4½" x 14½" rectangles for D.

e. Cut six 15½" x 19½" rectangles from the batting and backing fabric.

f. Cut ten 2" x 42" strips, or if you want a different binding for each place mat, cut two 2" x 42" strips from each fabric.

Appliqué Pieces

Appliqué patterns are on page 109.

2. You will need twelve peaches (E), and twelve each of leaves F and G. Read Machine Appliqué Using Fusible Web, page 95, to cut and prepare these pieces using appliqué templates and assorted yellow, pink, and green scraps of fabric.

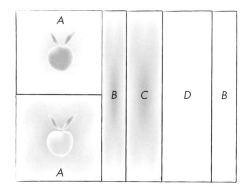

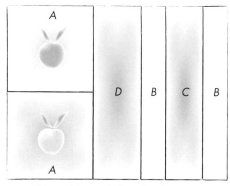

Place Mat with Peaches layouts

Place Mat with Peaches

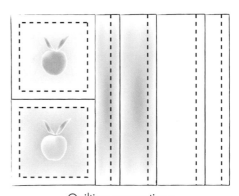

CONSTRUCTION

1. Follow the manufacturer's instructions and refer to the diagram below to position and fuse one peach E and one of leaf F and G to each A square as shown. Note that the leaves are close to the peach, but do not touch it. Make twelve blocks.

2. Using various colors of thread, sew all around the peaches and the leaves, very near to the edges, with a small running or zigzag stitch. Be sure to catch the background fabric to reinforce the pieces.

3. Refer to the *Place Mat with Peaches* layouts on page 56. Sew two Peach blocks together. Add the B, C, and D rectangles for each place mat in various fabric and block orders. Press seams open.

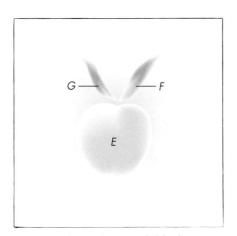

Make twelve Peach blocks

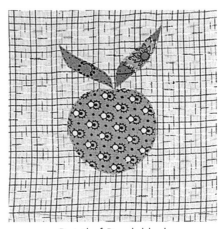

Detail of Peach block

QUILTING

1. Layer and baste each place mat, see page 99. Quilt as preferred by hand or machine, or follow our quilting suggestions.

2. Trim batting and backing even with the place mat. Sew the binding following the directions on page 99.

Quilting suggestions

Tote Bag

Tote bags in different sizes made by Marie-Christine Flocard, Beate Nellemann, and Cosabeth Parriaud.

Large: 15" x 20"
Medium: 12" x 16"

hese very useful tote bags are fun and fast to make, and are very convenient to use for shopping or to carry your quilting supplies. They also make a perfect gift for any occasion.

FABRIC SELECTION

Most of the fabrics selected are from the French company Les Olivades. One of the tote bags was made using American-made, Provençal-style fabric. See Sources, page 110. You can also choose piqué (textured fabric) or any other fabric.

FABRICS

Large Tote Bag

1 yard of fabric for bag and straps

1 yard of coordinating fabric for lining, straps, and pocket

¾ yard of fabric for backing

¾ yard Pellon or any thin batting

Medium Tote Bag

¾ yard of fabric for bag and straps

¾ yard of coordinating fabric for lining, straps, and pocket

½ yard of fabric for backing

½ yard Pellon or any thin batting

Other Materials

Graph paper for drawing pattern

tip
You can use a piece of muslin as the backing for your tote bag.

CUTTING

1. Draw pattern on paper using measurements on page 61.

2. Layer fabric, lining, backing, and batting.

3. Place bag pattern on top. Pin and cut the four layers as one. If you are using heavy fabric, cut one layer at a time.

4. Cut two 8" x 10½" pockets from the lining fabric for the large bag, or two 6½" x 8½" pockets for the medium bag.

5. For the large size bag, cut two 2¼" x 36" strips from the bag fabric and two 2¼" x 36" strips from the lining for the straps. For the medium size bag, cut two 2¼" x 34" strips each from bag fabric and lining.

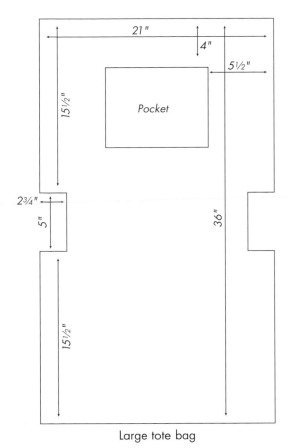

21"

4"

5½"

15½"

Pocket

2¾"

5"

36"

15½"

Large tote bag

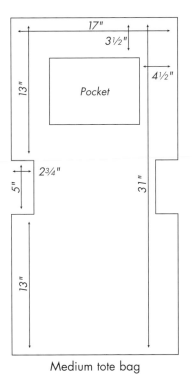

17"

3½"

4½"

13"

Pocket

2¾"

5"

31"

13"

Medium tote bag

tip

You can either trace the pattern on graph paper using the measurements given on this page or draw the tote bag directly on your fabric.

CONSTRUCTION

1. Layer fabric, batting, and backing. Pin or baste and machine quilt as preferred or shown below.

2. Mark straps and pocket placement on the lining.

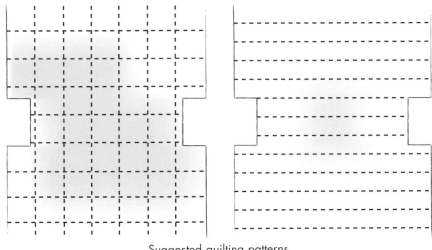

Suggested quilting patterns

Making the Pocket

3. Place right sides of the pocket pieces together; stitch all around, leaving an opening for turning.

4. Turn the pocket right side out. Hand stitch opening closed.

5. Place the pocket in the center of the lining and double stitch on three sides for added strength.

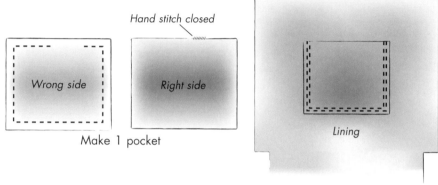

Hand stitch closed

Wrong side

Right side

Make 1 pocket

Lining

Double stitch around
outside of pocket

Making the Straps

6. Place one strip of bag fabric and one of lining fabric right sides together. Sew one long seam. Open and press.

7. Fold the sewn strips wrong sides together. Turn under ¼" on the unfinished long edges and topstitch.

8. Add a second row of topstitching.

9. Repeat double rows of topstitching on the opposite long edge.

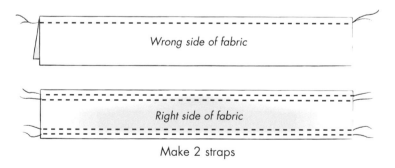

Wrong side of fabric

Right side of fabric

Make 2 straps

tip

You can appliqué a pieced block on the front of the tote bag. We used a leftover block from *Memories of Provence.*

Making the Bag

10. With right sides together sew the side seams together. Backstitch at beginning and end of seams.

11. Pinch the corners together so the side seam aligns with the bottom fold. Pin and sew, backstitching at the beginning and end of the seams. Reinforce seams with a second line of stitching. Turn bag right side out. Press.

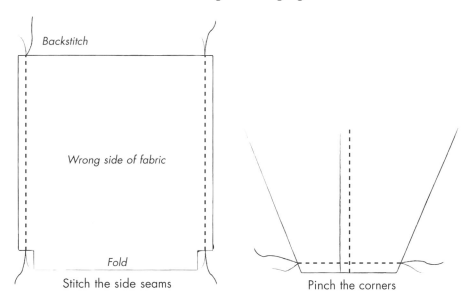

Backstitch

Wrong side of fabric

Fold

Stitch the side seams

Pinch the corners

Making the Lining

12. Place lining pieces right sides together and sew the side seams as if you were making a second bag. Leave an opening in one of the side seams for turning. Pinch the corners as described in step 11.

FINISHING

1. Pin straps in place on the right side of the bag on each side. Place lining and the bag right sides together.

2. Stitch 1/8"–1/4" from the edge around top of bag. Reinforce seams with a second row of stitching.

3. Turn tote bag right side out through the opening in the lining. Press the top seam and add a double row of topstitching. Press and hand stitch lining opening closed.

Wrong side of fabric

Place the straps between
bag and lining

Lavender Wand

*E*njoy making these lovely lavender wands for your linen drawers. In Provence they are called fusettes de lavande. They are easy to make from the lavender gathered late May or early June.

You will need:

- 38 fresh lavender stalks with long stems
- 2¾ yards narrow satin ribbon in your preferred color
- Scissors, clothespin, and a small safety pin

1. Tie the trimmed lavender stems in a neat bunch, just below the flower heads using narrow satin ribbon.

2. Turn the bunch upside down and gently fold the stems back until the flower heads are covered, following the illustration. Be sure the ribbon is always visible.

3. Attach a safety pin to the end of the ribbon, and weave the ribbon through the stalks, two at a time. Continue until the flower heads are covered. Secure ribbon with a clothespin.

4. Set aside for a week in a shaded area. Pull the woven ribbon to tighten up the wand. Wrap the remaining ribbon around the stems, saving some for the final knot and bow.

Menu du jour

VIN D'ORANGE
Delicious wine prepared with oranges.

❧❧

CAKE AUX OLIVES
Cake with olives to be served with *Vin d'Orange*.

❧❧

SALADE D'ORANGES ET D'OIGNONS
Refreshing orange salad with onions.
Can be served as an appetizer or with a main dish.

❧❧

TERRINE DE LÉGUMES D'ÉTÉ
Summer vegetable terrine.
Tasty appetizer served with a tomato coulis.

❧❧

AÏOLI
Traditional Provençal fish dish served with
fresh vegetables and a cold garlic sauce.

❧❧

ESTOUFFADE
Veal or lamb stew cooked in red wine,
served with garlic cream on toast.

❧❧

RATATOUILLE
Very popular Provençal vegetable dish.

❧❧

TOMATES PROVENÇALES
Side dish featuring baked tomatoes.

❧❧

CLAFOUTIS AUX ABRICOTS
Popular and easy-to-make dessert with apricots.

❧❧

PÊCHES AU VIN ROUGE À LA MENTHE FRAÎCHE
Tasty, beautiful dessert made with peaches in red wine with fresh mint.

❧❧

PAIN AU THYM
A hearty country bread made with thyme.

❧❧

ALL RECIPES SERVE FOUR PEOPLE

PROVENCE

Vin d'Orange
Orange Wine

Must be prepared well in advance.

This recipe was given to Marie-Christine by her friend Andrée who is from Antibes, on the Mediterranean coast near Nice. Make this wine when Seville or bitter oranges are in season.

6½ pounds Seville or other bitter oranges

1 quart inexpensive vodka with neutral taste

2¼ pounds (4 cups) sugar

5 bottles of dry wine—red, rosé, or white

1 vanilla bean—split

1. Remove the orange zest (but not the white pith). Put the zest in a glass jar, add the vodka, cover, and set aside for forty-five days.

2. After forty-five days, combine the zest/vodka mixture with the sugar, the wine, and the split vanilla bean. Stir and let sit covered for eight days.

3. After eight days, filter and bottle the liquid. Seal the bottles with good-quality corks and store in a cool area. You can start to drink it as an aperitif at room temperature or on ice after one month.

This recipe will yield approximately six 750 ml bottles.

The best season to find bitter oranges is winter.

Use the leftover oranges to prepare orange marmalade.

Cake aux Olives

Olive Cake

1 ½ cups flour

¼ ounce active dry yeast

4 eggs

⅓ cup olive oil

⅓ cup dry white wine

⅓ cup dry vermouth or port wine

½ teaspoon ground pepper

5 ounces (about ½ cup plus 2 tablespoons)
  total of green and black pitted olives

3½ ounces (about ½ cup) diced ham

3½ ounces (about ½ cup) diced red bell peppers

5 ounces (about ½ cup plus 2 tablespoons) grated Swiss cheese

¼ teaspoon salt (optional as olives, ham, and cheese are already salty)

Teflon-coated tube or loaf pan

Preheat oven to 350° F.

1. Mix the yeast and the flour in a large bowl.

2. Add the eggs and the olive oil. Stir with a wooden spoon.

3. Add the white wine and the ground pepper, and whip with an electric mixer. Add the vermouth or port.

4. Rinse the pitted olives under cold water. Cut them in half widthwise and add them to the bowl with the batter. Also add the red bell peppers, ham, and Swiss cheese. Add salt if desired. Mix with a wooden spoon.

5. Pour the mixture in a coated tube or loaf pan.

6. Bake for 1 ½ hours at 350° F.

Turn the cake onto a plate and let it cool. Cut in slices and serve with orange wine or your favorite beverage.

If you prefer, you can use ⅔ cup of one type of alcohol. For example, you can use either ⅔ cup of dry white wine, or vermouth, or port wine.

71

Salade d'Oranges et d'Oignons
Orange and Onion Salad

½ bunch Italian parsley

A few sprigs of basil

6 oranges

1–2 large onions—use fresh or new onions. If available, red onions add a nice color.

3–4 tablespoons olive oil

Salt and white pepper

1. Wash, dry, and chop parsley and basil.

2. Remove and grind the zest from one orange.

3. Peel the remaining oranges, carefully removing the white skin.

4. Cut oranges in thin slices. Save the juice.

5. Peel and cut onions in thin slices.

6. Arrange oranges and onions in a large salad bowl or on a large plate. Add the chopped parsley and basil, olive oil, the orange juice and zest, and salt and pepper to taste.

7. Mix all ingredients gently in order not to break the fruit.

8. Place in the refrigerator for at least two hours.
Remove ½ hour before serving.

To reduce some of the strong onion taste, let onions marinate in advance with the oranges, the orange juice, and the olive oil.

Terrine de Légumes d'Été

Summer Vegetable Terrine

6 tablespoons olive oil

1 medium eggplant

1 zucchini

3 seeded and diced tomatoes

1 sliced onion

2 chopped bell peppers (one green, one yellow)

6 eggs

3 tablespoons chopped fresh basil leaves

1 tablespoon chopped fresh parsley

2 crushed garlic cloves

Salt and pepper

1 lemon

10" Teflon-coated baking pan

1. Preheat oven to 375° F.

2. Rinse and thinly slice the unpeeled eggplant and zucchini.

3. Sauté the eggplant and the zucchini over medium heat in a frying pan with two tablespoons of olive oil until golden, about five to ten minutes.

4. In another frying pan, slowly cook the seeded and diced tomatoes, sliced onion, and chopped bell peppers in two tablespoons of olive oil. Cook for about ten minutes.

5. Place one layer of eggplant and one of zucchini in the coated baking pan. Spread six tablespoons of the red mixture (tomatoes, onion, and bell peppers). Repeat the layers until all vegetables and red mixture have been used.

6. In a bowl, beat the eggs with the basil, parsley, and crushed garlic. Pour over the vegetables and red mixture, and cover with aluminum foil. Cook for an hour in a water bath in the 375° F oven.

Place your baking pan in a roasting pan with one cup of cold water. The water bath will keep the terrine moist.

(continued on next page)

7. Remove the foil and bake for another twenty minutes.

8. Cover and chill the cooked terrine in the refrigerator for several hours before serving.

9. To serve, turn the terrine out of the baking pan, and cut in slices. Salt and pepper to taste. Serve with olive oil and lemon juice. You can also serve it with a tomato coulis.

You can prepare this terrine a day in advance and keep it covered in the refrigerator.

Coulis de Tomates

Tomato Sauce (Makes 2 cups)

1 chopped onion

1 tablespoon olive oil

6–8 tomatoes

1 tablespoon tomato paste

1 tablespoon powdered sugar

1 sprig parsley—minced

1. Sauté the onion in olive oil until transparent.

2. Peel, seed, and dice the tomatoes, then mash them on a plate with a fork. Add the mashed tomatoes to the onion, along with the tomato paste and the sugar.

3. Cover and cook gently for 15–20 minutes, so that it is not too liquid. Purée in a blender, and let cool. Decorate with minced parsley.

Aïoli

Aïoli is the name for both the garlic sauce and the dish. Traditionally, the sauce is made with a mortar and a pestle. If you prefer, make it with an wire whisk or electric mixer.

1 quart fish broth

2 pounds fresh cod or other white fish such as monkfish or halibut

9 small potatoes

8 small carrots

4 small artichokes

1 pound French green beans

1 cauliflower

4 tomatoes

5 eggs

Salt and pepper

3–4 cloves of garlic

¾–1 cup olive oil

If you find the taste of olive oil too strong, mix it 50/50 with another milder oil.

Potatoes, carrots, artichokes, French green beans (*haricots verts*), cauliflower, and tomatoes are used in the traditional recipe. However, you can add or substitute any vegetables you like, such as fennel, onions, zucchini, and so on.

1. Poach fish in fish broth until firm and opaque, about 10 minutes. Remove from heat and keep warm.

2. Each vegetable (potatoes, carrots, artichokes, green beans, and cauliflower) has a different cooking time—so prepare and cook each separately to keep crunchy—except for the potatoes which should be cooked until soft. Cook vegetables whole. Do not cook tomatoes.

3. Hard-boil four eggs for ten minutes, and chill under cold water.

Meanwhile, prepare the sauce:

4. Peel and mash garlic in the mortar with the pestle until creamy or use a garlic press.

5. Mash half of one cooked potato on a plate and add to the garlic.

6. Add one raw egg yolk, salt, and pepper.

7. Start adding olive oil in a thin stream, little by little, whisking well by hand or using an electric mixer (as with making mayonnaise). Add salt and pepper to taste.

8. Arrange all ingredients nicely on a serving plate: fish in the center and vegetables all around, with halved hard-boiled eggs and tomatoes. Serve with the sauce.

for a successful sauce, be sure the egg yolk and oil are at room temperature.

Estouffade
Veal or Lamb Stew

2½ pounds boneless lamb (leg or shoulder)
or veal shoulder, cut into 1" cubes

3 peeled, seeded, and diced tomatoes

1 large chopped onion

3 cloves garlic

Peel of one orange

1 sliced celery stalk

Bouquet garni or 2 tablespoons herbes de Provence

1 bottle red wine

3 tablespoons olive oil

1 tablespoon freshly ground pepper

1 tablespoon salt

½ pound diced bacon (or pork-back fat)

6 ounces pork rind

2 beef broth cubes

1. Place meat, tomatoes, chopped onion, garlic cloves, orange peel,
celery, bouquet garni, salt and pepper in a casserole dish. Add the wine
and olive oil. Marinate for four hours in a cool place.

2. Add the diced bacon or back fat, the pork rind, and beef broth cubes.
Cook slowly in a covered pot on top of the stove at medium temperature
for two hours. If you have too much liquid, remove the lid and meat and
continue cooking until the sauce has reduced to the desired consistency.

You can serve this dish with fresh pasta or rice, and ratatouille, page 82,
or Tomates Provençales, page 85.

You can also prepare this dish in the oven in a clay pot. In this case, the
liquid should completely cover the meat so you may have to add cold water.
Place in a preheated oven and cook covered for three hours at a very low
temperature (275° F).

GARLIC CREAM ON TOASTED BREAD

1 garlic bulb

2 tablespoons olive oil

½ baguette

*Peel the garlic cloves. To reduce the strong
flavor place them in two cups of boiling
water for five minutes and drain. Repeat
four times. Place them with the olive oil
in a food processor or a mortar. Process
or mash them.*

*Cut thin slices of the baguette and toast
them lightly. Spread the garlic cream on the
toast. Re-toast in the oven and serve with
the estouffade.*

Ratatouille

This is a traditional Provençal recipe. You can serve it cold or warm with lamb, chicken, or pork. It is also a great addition to a barbecue.

The secret of this dish is to cook all the vegetables separately before combining them.

3 green squash/zucchini

2 eggplants

¾ cup olive oil

4 large tomatoes (well-ripened)

2 medium onions

2 peppers (green, yellow, or red)

4 garlic cloves

1 tablespoon thyme or herbes de Provence

1 bay leaf

1. Wash and dice the squash/zucchini and the eggplants. Do not peel them.

2. Drop the tomatoes in a pan of boiling water for twenty seconds. Rinse with cold water. Peel and seed them.

3. Sauté the onions in three tablespoons of olive oil until transparent. Put them on a plate.

4. Sauté the vegetables separately, using about two tablespoons of olive oil for each.

5. Pour two to three tablespoons of olive oil into a clean frying pan. Mix the vegetables together, and add with three crushed garlic cloves, thyme, and bay leaf to frying pan.

6. Cover and cook slowly for approximately forty minutes. Just before serving crush the last garlic clove to add a fresh taste of garlic to the dish.

Tomates Provençales

In Provence, a tomato is also called *pomme d'amour*, and in Italy, *pomodore*. Choose good-quality, firm tomatoes for this dish.

These tomatoes go well with meat and fish recipes.

4 large firm, red tomatoes (or 8 small ones)

Salt and pepper

2–4 garlic cloves

1 bunch parsley

¼–⅓ cup olive oil

½ tablespoon powdered sugar (to reduce acidity)

4 tablespoons bread crumbs

1. Preheat oven to 325° F.

2. Cut the tomatoes in half, remove seeds, and sprinkle lightly with salt. Turn them upside down in a sieve or drain on paper towels for about fifteen minutes.

3. Peel and mince garlic. Wash, dry, and chop parsley.

4. Heat half of the olive oil in a large frying pan. When hot, add tomatoes, and cook for five minutes. Turn them and cook for another five minutes.

5. Place tomatoes cut side up in a lightly oiled dish, just large enough to hold them. Sprinkle with salt, pepper, and sugar. Add garlic, parsley, and breadcrumbs. Sprinkle with the remaining olive oil.

6. Bake for about one hour at 325° F. Don't let the tomatoes darken— shorten cooking time if necessary, or cover with aluminum foil.

Clafoutis aux Abricots
Apricot Clafoutis

4 tablespoons flour

6 tablespoons sugar

1 teaspoon salt

3 large eggs

⅓ cup milk

⅓ cup whipping cream

2 tablespoons melted butter

1 teaspoon vanilla extract or powder

1¼ pounds ripe apricots or one 32-ounce can apricots in light syrup

1. Preheat oven to 375° F.

2. Combine flour, sugar, salt, and eggs in a bowl. Add the milk and whipping cream while stirring with an electric mixer or wire whisk. The batter must be very smooth, without lumps.

3. Add the melted butter and vanilla.

4. If using fresh apricots, wash and cut them in half. Remove the pits.

5. Place the apricots cut side down in a greased baking dish. Pour the batter over the fruit.

6. Bake 40–45 minutes at 375° F oven.

If you like a sweet taste you can add some confectioner's sugar just before serving. You may also add some toasted, sliced almonds.

You can replace apricots with other fruits such as nectarines, pears, or peaches.

Pêches au Vin Rouge à la Menthe Fraîche

Peaches Cooked in Red Wine with Fresh Mint

1 bunch fresh mint leaves

4 large peaches (or 8 small ones)

1 bottle red wine

½ pound (1 cup) powdered sugar

1. Rinse and dry the mint. Save some small, nice leaves for decoration.

2. Peel the peaches carefully.

3. Pour wine, sugar, and mint in a saucepan. Stir. Bring to boil.

4. Add the peaches to the simmering liquid and poach for about ten to fifteen minutes (depending on the ripeness of the peaches), until they become tender. If the peaches are not covered with wine, you might need to turn them halfway. Remove the peaches from the saucepan, and place on a nice serving plate.

5. Let the mint wine simmer for another 20–30 minutes to reduce it to thin syrup. Cool the liquid, and remove the mint leaves before pouring over the peaches.

6. Garnish with a mint leaf on top of each peach and serve cool, not cold.

7. Drizzle one or two tablespoons of syrup on fruit just before serving for a shiny look.

This tasty dessert is not only easy and fast to make, but it tastes heavenly and looks lovely with its deep red color.

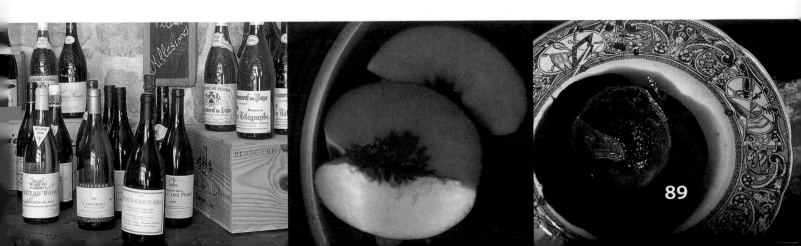

89

Pain au Thyme

Thyme Bread

Makes one 5" x 9" loaf.

¼ ounce active dry yeast

1½ cups lukewarm water (100° F–110° F)

4½–5 cups flour

1 tablespoon thyme or herbes de Provence

½–1 teaspoon salt

Preheat oven to 400° F.

1. Combine yeast and water in a large bowl. Add flour, herbs, and salt. Knead briefly.

2. Cover with a towel, and allow the dough to rise in a warm place, for approximately one hour, or until the dough has doubled.

3. Knead briefly, then let the dough rise and double a second time.

4. Knead for five to ten minutes. Shape dough into a loaf. Place on a lightly greased cooking sheet. Cut some crisscrosses with a knife.

5. Bake for 45 minutes.

Herbes de Provence are used in many different recipes. They are thyme, wild thyme, sage, basil, rosemary, marjoram, oregano, and savory.

90

General instructions

FABRIC

Use 100% cotton. We recommend prewashing all of your fabrics (except for the *Boutis Provençal*, page 23), especially if you are planning to make a tablecloth, place mats, or a bed-size quilt that will require laundering.

Wash darks and lights separately by hand, or using the soak cycle on your machine; then machine dry on the permanent-press setting. Some quilters also feel that prewashing eliminates the chemicals used in the fabric printing process, making the fabrics softer and therefore easier to work with, particularly when hand quilting.

Fabric requirements are based on 42"-wide fabrics unless otherwise stated. Be aware that many fabrics shrink when washed, and widths vary by manufacturer. Cut strips on the crosswise grain unless otherwise specified.

SUPPLIES

You need the following supplies to make the various quilts and projects in this book:

Lavender is an aromatic plant that comes from Persia and the Canary Islands. The Romans introduced it in Provence in antiquity. Used in the past for its healing virtue, it is mostly appreciated nowadays for its perfume.

- Sewing machine in good working order. It is always a good idea to start any new project with a new needle.
- Cotton sewing and quilting threads to match fabrics
- Scissors (fabric and paper)
- Iron and ironing board
- Pins
- Spray adhesive or safety pins for basting
- Template material
- Freezer paper (for appliqué)
- Fusible web
- Seam ripper
- 6" x 24" rectangular, a Bias Square, and 15"-square see-through acrylic rulers
- Rotary cutter and mat
- Marking tools
- Design wall: can be a flannel-backed tablecloth or a piece of cotton batting tacked to the wall

Marseille Soap (Savon de Marseille) originated in Provence and dates back to the Middle Ages. The city of Marseille became the first official soap manufacturer in France in the sixteenth century. Authentic Marseille soap is 100% natural. It must contain 72% oil—olive oil which has been used since the beginning, or other vegetable oils such as palm tree oil and copra oil. Because it does not contain any coloring or artificial additives, this soap is good for the skin and is also recommended for washing clothes. We use it for washing our quilts.

Marseille soap

SEAM ALLOWANCES

Use ¼" for all pieced projects. It's a good idea to do a test seam before you begin sewing to check for accuracy.

PRESSING

Press seams toward the darker fabric unless otherwise noted. Press lightly in an up-and-down motion. Avoid using a very hot iron or over-pressing, both of which can distort pieces and blocks. Use a dry iron to prevent seam allowances from marking top fabric.

APPLIQUÉ
Hand Appliqué Method One

1. Trace around your chosen template onto the wrong side of the appliqué fabric. Do not cut yet. Place the fabric on top of several layers of fabric scraps for cushioning. Using a sharp, thick pin or needle—embroidery needles work well—press firmly following the traced line to create a fine line or furrow.

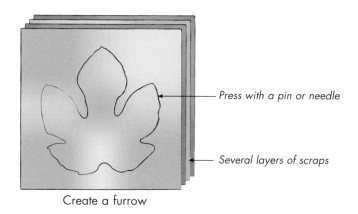

Press with a pin or needle

Several layers of scraps

Create a furrow

2. Cut out leaving 3⁄16"-¼" turn-under allowance. After cutting the points and clipping the concave curves you will find it very easy to baste or pin as the fabric folds naturally with the furrow.

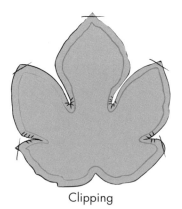

Clipping

3. Be careful when folding the points. To create a sharp point, fold the fabric tip down as shown in Step A. Fold one edge and then the other to make a point as shown in Steps B and C. Baste in place, and appliqué using your preferred stitch.

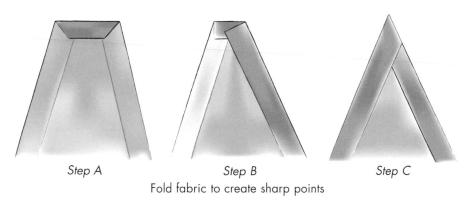

Step A   *Step B*   *Step C*

Fold fabric to create sharp points

Hand Appliqué Method Two: Freezer Paper Appliqué

1. Draw the pattern on the paper side of the freezer paper. Cut out the shape following the line. Lay the freezer paper template, shiny side down, on the wrong side of your appliqué fabric. Press with a hot iron for a few seconds. Cut fabric allowing 3/16"–1/4" to turn under.

2. Clip the concave curves. You will see that the fabric will easily fold over the paper. Baste the piece all around, through fabric and paper. You can also secure the seam allowance with a fabric glue stick to avoid having to baste with thread. Appliqué using your preferred stitch.

3. Remove the basting stitches and paper before you have appliquéd the piece entirely, using tweezers to pull out the freezer paper (Method A). You may also appliqué the piece completely and remove the freezer paper by making a thin slit in the background fabric behind the appliqué. Be sure not to cut the appliqué fabric! Remove the basting stitches, then use tweezers to remove the freezer paper (Method B).

Machine Appliqué Using Fusible Web

1. Use a pencil to trace the appliqué designs onto the paper side of the fusible web. Remember to reverse the design if necessary.

2. Use paper-cutting scissors to cut out the pieces, leaving about 1/4" beyond your traced lines.

METHOD A

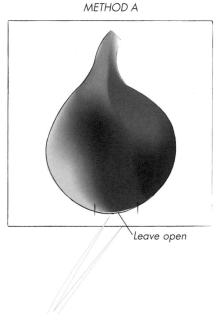

Leave open

METHOD B

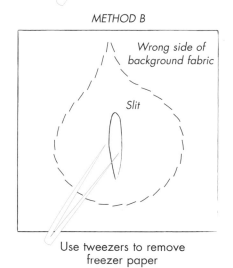

Wrong side of background fabric

Slit

Use tweezers to remove freezer paper

3. Follow the manufacturer's instructions to fuse the cut-out web to the wrong side of the appliqué fabric. Use a pressing sheet to protect your iron and ironing board from excess adhesive.

4. Cut the fabric along the traced pencil lines. Remove the paper backing and press the fabric shapes in place, following the manufacturer's instructions. If you have trouble removing the paper backing, use a pin to score the paper. You can leave the edges raw, or strengthen them using running, buttonhole, or satin stitching.

FABRIC PAINTING

Painting fabric is not difficult, and it is so pleasant to play with colors.

Prepare the colors that you will use for painting. If you only have the paints in primary colors (yellow, red, and blue) plus black and white, mix them to create your own palette. For example: mix yellow and red to create orange, or blue and red to create purple.

To obtain blue-green, first combine yellow and blue to create green, and then add more blue. To create yellow-green, add some more yellow to the green color.

Add white to create light values. Add black to create darker values. (For example, brown—a darker shade of orange—is made by mixing orange with black.) Add a touch of gray to create different tones.

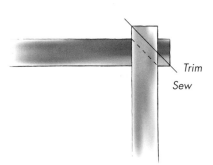

Trim
Sew

Place border strips right sides together at right angles. Stitch diagonally from corner to corner.

Press seams open

Practice and experiment on a piece of fabric before painting your appliqué pieces. Don't use too much water or the color will run on the fabric. Add details with undiluted paint, using a thin brush.

Remember: Practice!

BORDERS

Borders for the projects in this book have either straight-cut or mitered corners. Border strips are cut on the crosswise grain unless otherwise noted. If necessary, piece the strips together with a diagonal seam to create the needed lengths.

BORDERS WITH STRAIGHT-CUT CORNERS

Unless otherwise noted, the side borders are sewn on first. When you have finished the quilt top, measure it down the center vertically. This is the length to cut the side borders.

Place pins at the centers and quarter points of the sides of the quilt top, and do the same with each side border strip. Pin the borders to the quilt top, matching the pins. Sew the borders to the quilt top using a ¼" seam allowance, and press seams toward the border. Measure side to side through the center of the quilt, including the side borders. This is the length to cut the top and bottom borders. Repeat pinning, sewing, and pressing to add the top and bottom borders to the quilt.

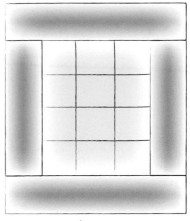

Straight-cut corners

BORDERS WITH MITERED CORNERS

Vanne Provençale (page 35) and *Fig Tree Leaves* (page 16) have borders with mitered corners.

1. Determine the finished outside dimensions (length and width) of your quilt, including borders.

2. Cut border strips to these lengths plus at least ½" for seam allowance. For extra insurance add 2"–3" to give yourself some leeway.

3. Mark the centers of the quilt top edges and border strips. Pin the borders to the quilt top, matching centers. Sew the border strips to the quilt top using a ¼" seam allowance. Each border should extend the same distance beyond each end of the quilt top. Start and stop sewing ¼" from the corners of the quilt top. Press seams toward the borders.

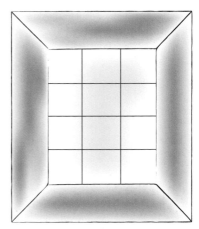

Mitered corners

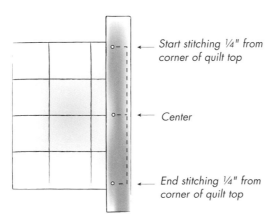

Start stitching ¼" from corner of quilt top

Center

End stitching ¼" from corner of quilt top

4. Lay the first corner to be mitered on the ironing board. Fold the top strip under at a 45° angle, and adjust so raw edges match perfectly. Press.

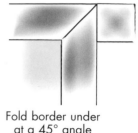

Fold border under
at a 45° angle

5. Carefully fold the quilt following the diagonal with right sides together, lining up the border edges. If necessary, use a ruler to draw a pencil line on the crease to make it more visible. Sew on the pressed crease, starting at the inside corner and sewing to the outside edge.

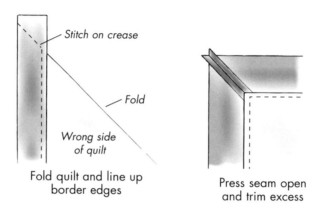

Stitch on crease

Fold

Wrong side
of quilt

Fold quilt and line up
border edges

Press seam open
and trim excess

6. Press the seam open and trim away excess border strips, leaving a ¼" seam allowance. Repeat for the three remaining corners.

BACKING

Make the backing 2"–4" larger than the quilt top on all sides. Prewash the fabric, and trim the selvages.

To economize, you can piece the back from any leftover fabrics or blocks.

BATTING

The type of batting you use is a personal decision. For a more traditional look, consider using a very thin cotton batting and then washing the quilt after you have finished quilting it. Some cotton battings can be purchased by the yard; consult your local quilt shop for options. Whatever batting you use, cut it 2"–4" larger than your quilt top on all sides.

fact

Did you know that "blue denim" was created in Nîmes, Provence? In France, *le bleu de Nîmes*, a very strong cotton fabric, was used for making clothes for workers.

LAYERING

Spread the backing wrong side up, and tape the edges down with masking tape. (If you are working on a carpet you can use T-pins to secure the backing to the carpet.) Center the batting over the backing, and smooth out any folds. Place the quilt top right side up on top of the batting and backing, making sure it is centered.

BASTING

If you plan to machine quilt, baste the layers together with safety pins placed a maximum of 3" apart. Begin basting in the center and move toward the edges first in vertical, then horizontal rows.

We love the adhesive spray for basting. It is fast, it secures both smaller and larger works, and there are no pins in your way when you are quilting.

If you plan to hand quilt, baste the layers together with a long needle and light-colored thread. Begin in the center and move out toward the edges, making the stitches approximately the length of the needle.

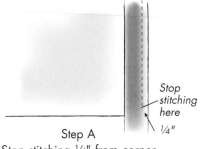

Step A
Stop stitching ¼" from corner

QUILTING

Quilting, by hand or machine, enhances the pieced or appliquéd design of the quilt. You may choose to quilt in-the-ditch, echo the pieced or appliqué motifs, use patterns from quilting design books and stencils, or create your own free-motion quilting design. Quilting suggestions are included for each project.

BINDING (DOUBLE FOLD)

1. Trim excess batting and backing even with the quilt top. For a ¼" finished double fold binding, cut fabric strips 2" wide and piece them together with a diagonal seam to make a continuous binding strip (see page 100). Press the seams open.

2. Press the entire strip in half lengthwise with wrong sides together. With raw edges even, pin the binding to the edge of the quilt a few inches from a corner. Leave the first few inches of the binding unattached, and start sewing, using a ¼" seam allowance.

3. Stop ¼" from the first corner and backstitch one stitch (Step A). Cut the thread. Lift the presser foot and rotate the quilt. Fold the binding at a 45°

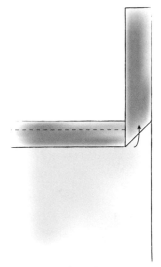

Step B
Fold binding up at 45° angle

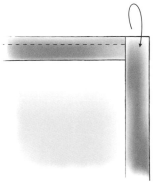

Step C
Fold binding down

angle so it extends straight above the quilt (Step B). Then bring the binding strip down even with the edge of the quilt. Begin sewing at the folded edge (Step C).

4. Repeat for the remaining corners.

5. To finish the binding, trim the starting and ending ends of the binding at a 45° angle, allowing a 1" overlap. Fold one end under (to provide a finished edge) and finish stitiching the binding to the quilt.

Continuous Bias Binding

The continuous bias method allows you to cut a single long bias strip to use for binding or piping. Quilts with curved edges require bias binding.

1. Begin by cutting a square of fabric. For example, if yardage is ½ yard, cut an 18" square. Cut the square in half diagonally, creating two triangles.

2. Sew these triangles right sides together as shown in Step A. Use a ¼" seam allowance and press the seam open.

3. Use a ruler to mark the fabric parallelogram with lines spaced the width of your bias strip (Step B). Cut along the first line about 5".

4. Pin Side 1 and Side 2 right sides together to form a tube. Align A with the raw edge at B (Step C). This will allow the first line to be offset by one strip width. Pin the ends together, making sure that the lines match. Sew with a ¼" seam allowance. Cut along the lines and press seams open.

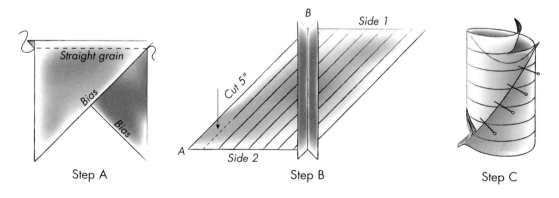

Step A   Step B   Step C

Project
Patterns

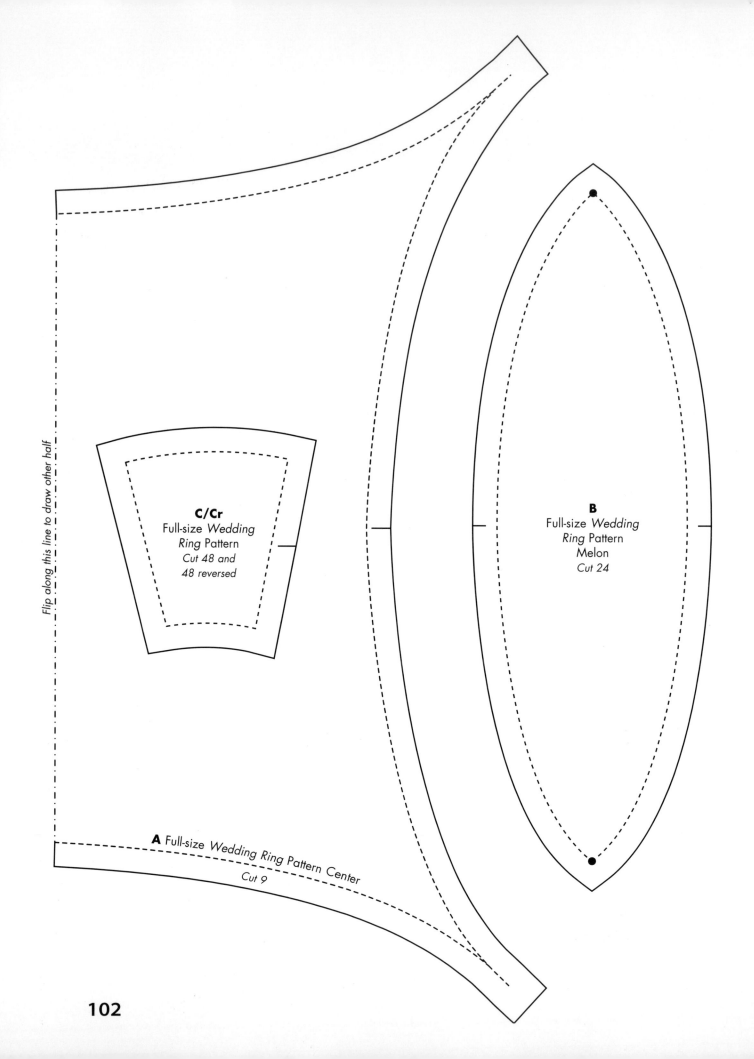

Flip along this line to draw other half

C/Cr
Full-size *Wedding
Ring* Pattern
*Cut 48 and
48 reversed*

A Full-size Wedding Ring Pattern Center
Cut 9

B
Full-size *Wedding
Ring* Pattern
Melon
Cut 24

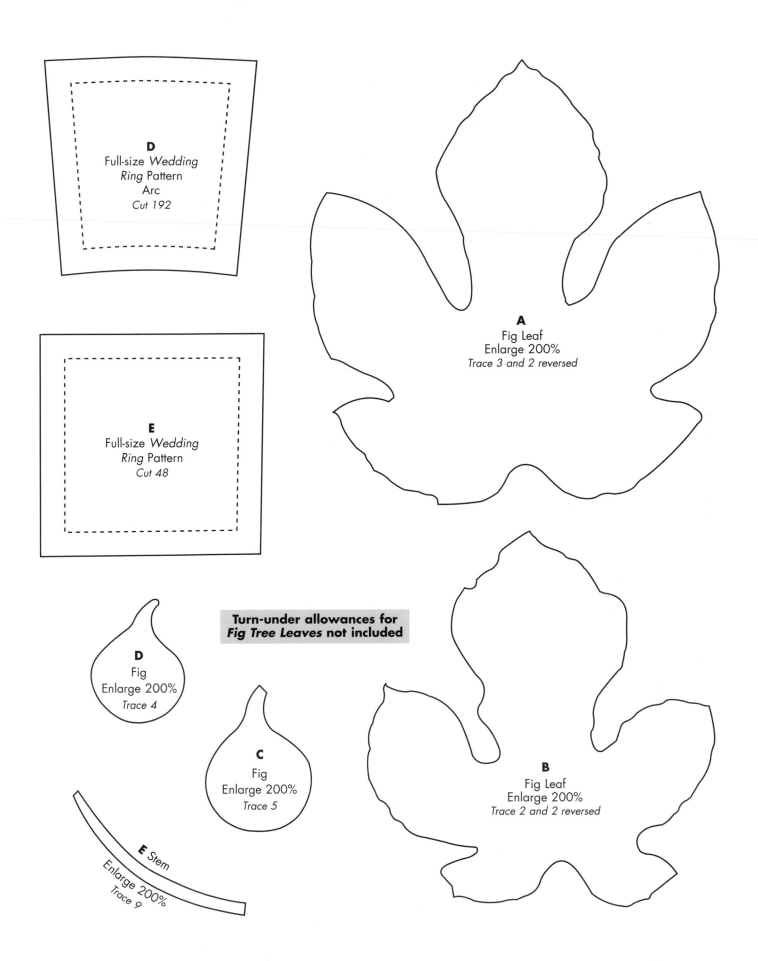

D
Full-size *Wedding Ring* Pattern
Arc
Cut 192

E
Full-size *Wedding Ring* Pattern
Cut 48

A
Fig Leaf
Enlarge 200%
Trace 3 and 2 reversed

Turn-under allowances for *Fig Tree Leaves* not included

D
Fig
Enlarge 200%
Trace 4

C
Fig
Enlarge 200%
Trace 5

E Stem
Enlarge 200%
Trace 9

B
Fig Leaf
Enlarge 200%
Trace 2 and 2 reversed

Boutis Provençal central motif
Enlarge 250% to 18⅜" x 18⅜"

Full-size
Vanne Provençale Pattern
first inner border

Full-size *Vanne Provençale* Pattern second border

Full-size *Vanne Provençale* Pattern second border

105

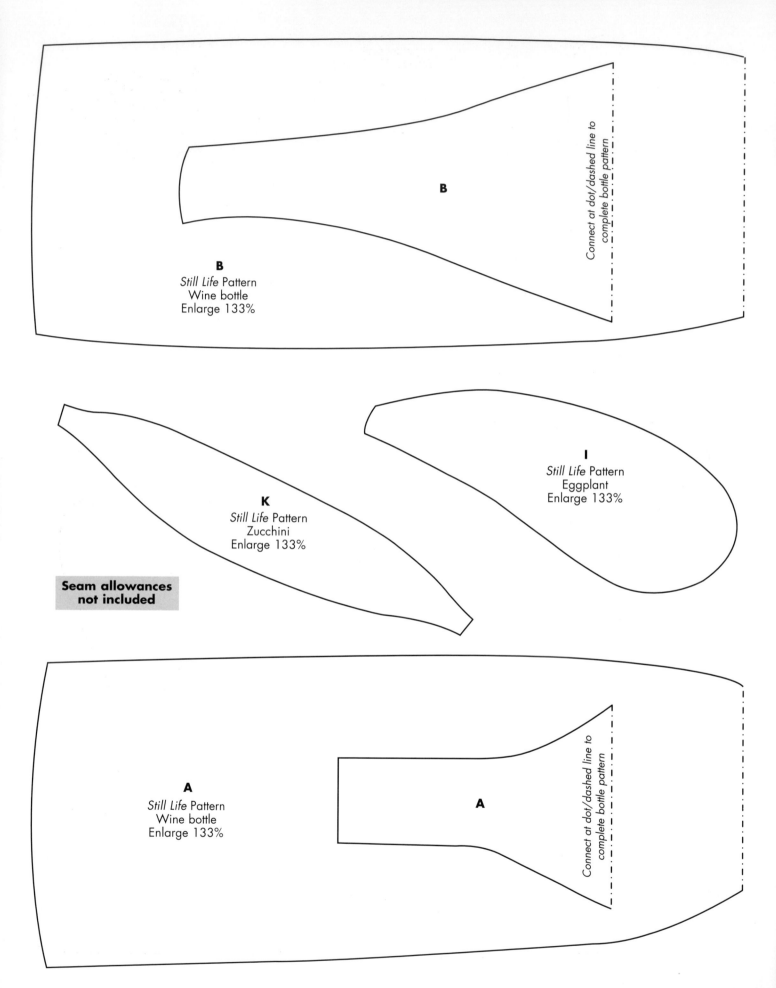

B

Still Life Pattern
Wine bottle
Enlarge 133%

B

Connect at dot/dashed line to complete bottle pattern

K

Still Life Pattern
Zucchini
Enlarge 133%

I

Still Life Pattern
Eggplant
Enlarge 133%

**Seam allowances
not included**

A

Still Life Pattern
Wine bottle
Enlarge 133%

A

Connect at dot/dashed line to complete bottle pattern

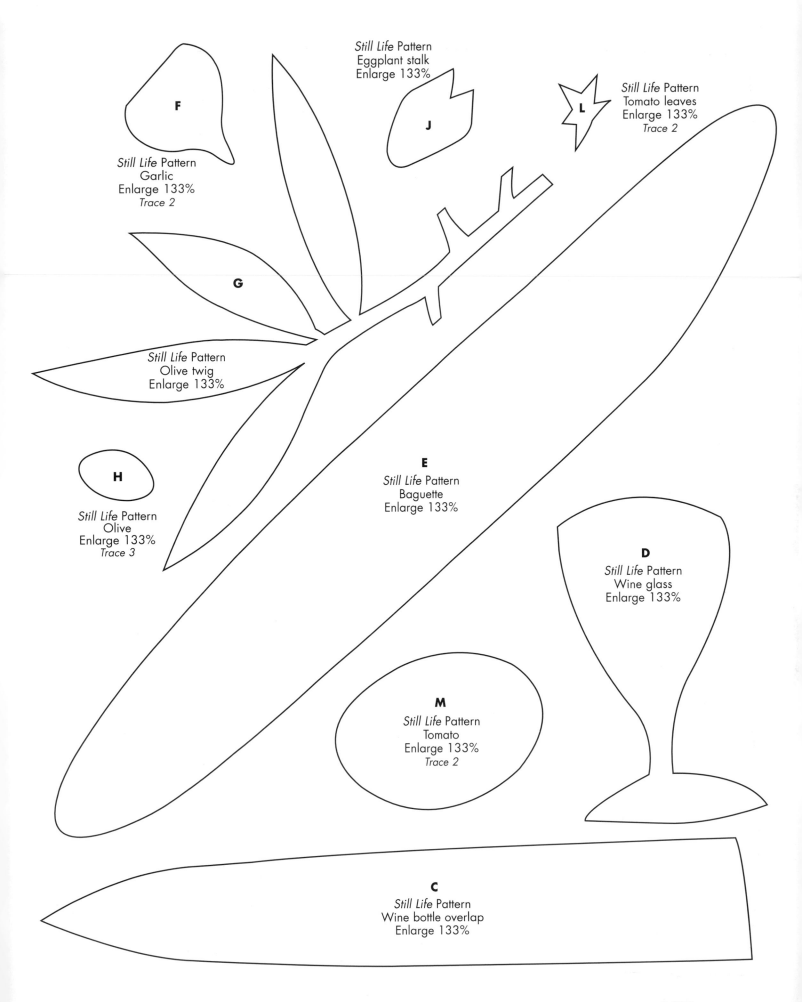

Still Life Pattern
Garlic
Enlarge 133%
Trace 2

Still Life Pattern
Eggplant stalk
Enlarge 133%

Still Life Pattern
Tomato leaves
Enlarge 133%
Trace 2

Still Life Pattern
Olive twig
Enlarge 133%

Still Life Pattern
Olive
Enlarge 133%
Trace 3

Still Life Pattern
Baguette
Enlarge 133%

Still Life Pattern
Wine glass
Enlarge 133%

Still Life Pattern
Tomato
Enlarge 133%
Trace 2

Still Life Pattern
Wine bottle overlap
Enlarge 133%

F

J

L

G

H

E

D

M

C

107

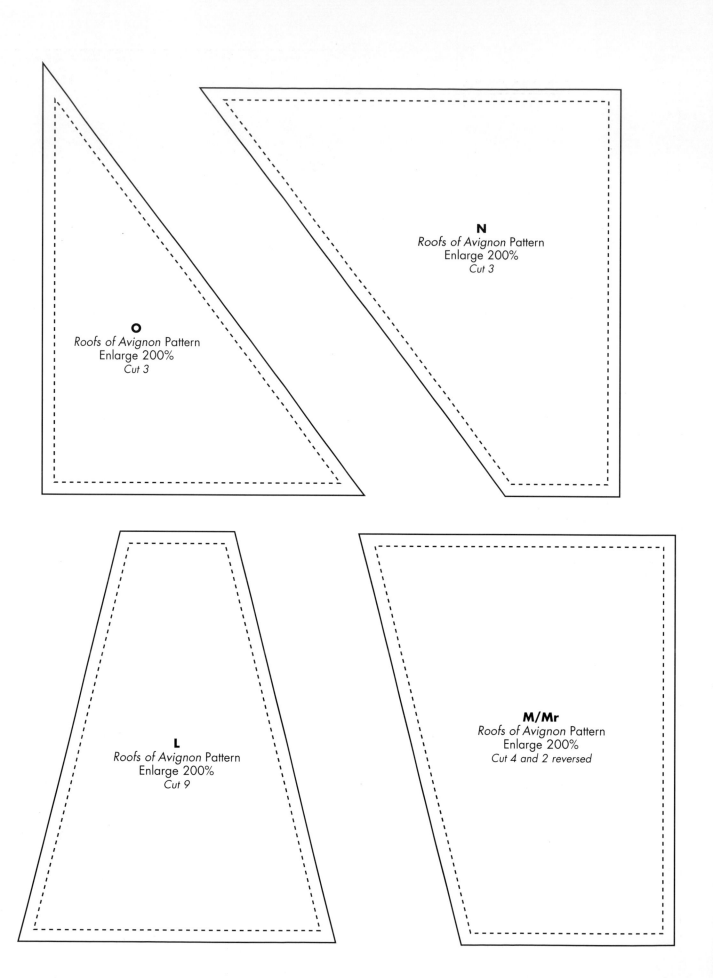

N
Roofs of Avignon Pattern
Enlarge 200%
Cut 3

O
Roofs of Avignon Pattern
Enlarge 200%
Cut 3

L
Roofs of Avignon Pattern
Enlarge 200%
Cut 9

M/Mr
Roofs of Avignon Pattern
Enlarge 200%
Cut 4 and 2 reversed

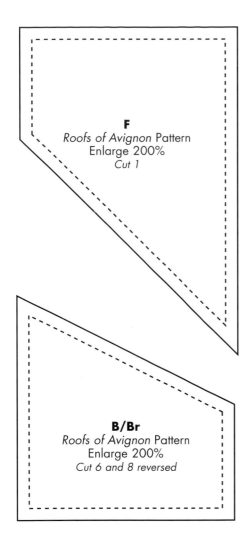

F
Roofs of Avignon Pattern
Enlarge 200%
Cut 1

B/Br
Roofs of Avignon Pattern
Enlarge 200%
Cut 6 and 8 reversed

C
Roofs of Avignon Pattern
Enlarge 200%
Cut 10

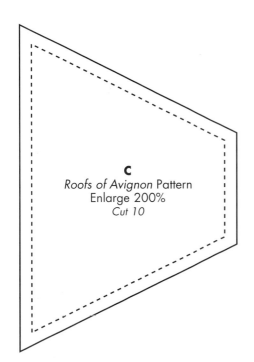

K/Kr
Roofs of Avignon Pattern
Enlarge 200%
Cut 5 and 5 reversed

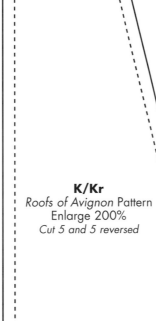

Still Life with bottles and fruit

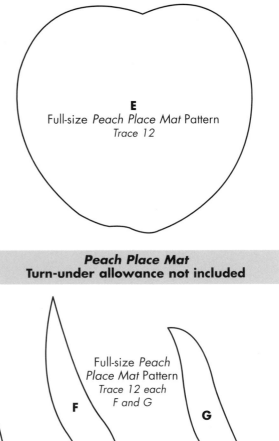

E
Full-size *Peach Place Mat* Pattern
Trace 12

Peach Place Mat
Turn-under allowance not included

Full-size *Peach Place Mat* Pattern
Trace 12 each F and G

F

G

109

P R O V E N C E

$\mathcal{S}$ources

Fabric and Quilting Supplies

CHERRYWOOD FABRICS
P.O. Box 486
Brainerd, MN 56401
Phone: 888-296-0967
Hand-dyed suede-look cotton
www.cherrywoodfabrics.com

CLOTILDE
Phone: 800-772-2891
www.clotilde.com

COTTON PATCH MAIL ORDER
3405 Hall Lane, Dept. CTB
Lafayette, CA 94549
Phone: 800-835-4418 or
925-283-7883
www.quiltusa.com
Email: quiltusa@aol.com
Fabrics and quilt supplies

DEN HAAN AND WAGENMAKERS
N.Z. Voorburgwal 97-99
1012 RE Amsterdam, Netherlands
www.dutchquilts.com
Email: dhaanwag@xs4all.nl
*Dutch fabric selection, old toile,
and Provençal print reproductions*

NANCY'S NOTIONS
Phone: 800-833-0690
www.nancysnotions.com

POPPY FABRIC
5151 Broadway
Oakland, CA 94611
Phone: 800-55-POPPY
A large selection of Provençal fabrics

LE ROUVRAY
3 Rue de la Bûcherie
F-75005 Paris, France
Phone: 011-33-1-43-25-00-45
Fax: 011-33-1-43-25-51-61
www.lerouvray.com
*A large selection of French fabrics
from Provence, and toiles de Jouy*

LES OLIVADES
Chemin des Indienneurs
F-13103 Saint Etienne du Grès,
France
Phone: 011-33-4-90-49-19-19
Fax: 011-33-4-90-49-19-20
www.olivades.fr
Provençal fabrics and accessories

Photo Transfer

IMAGINATION STATION
7571 Crater Lake Highway
Suite #101
White City, OR 97503
Phone: 541-826-7954 or
800-338-3857
Photo transfer services

FABRIC FOTOS
3801 Olsen #3
Amarillo, TX 79108
Phone: 806-359-8241
Photo transfer services

THE STITCHIN' POST
P.O. Box 280
Sisters, OR 97759
www.stitchinpost.com
Email: stitchin@stitchinpost.com
Phone: 541-549-6061
*Photo transfer services
Write or call in advance.*

DHARMA TRADING CO.
Phone: 800-542-5227
www.dharmatrading.com
*Fabric paints, photo transfer paper,
and other photo transfer materials*

Reference Book

Jean Ray Laury: *The Photo Transfer
Handbook*, C&T Publishing, Inc.
Lafayette, California
www.ctpub.com

Miscellaneous Information on Provence

LA SÉRÉNITÉ
Bed & Breakfast
F-30430 Barjac, France
Phone: 011-33-4-66-24-54-63

Michelin: *The Green Guide Provence*
Travel publications
www.michelin-travel.com

POTERIE LE CHÊNE VERT
Boisset & Gaujac
Route d'Alès
F-30140 Anduze, France
Phone: 011-33-4-66-61-70-24
Fax: 011-33-4-66-61-70-71
www.poterie-anduze.com
*Famous Anduze pottery,
see page 27.*

Marie-Christine Flocard (left) and Cosabeth Parriaud

*F*ifteen years ago Marie-Christine and Cosabeth met at Le Rouvray in Paris, a leading quilt shop in France. Besides sharing their passions for quilts and cuisine they have also written books together in French and English.

Marie-Christine discovered patchwork while living in Berkeley, CA in 1976. She went from being an elementary school teacher to focusing exclusively on quilts. She is in charge of organizing all the workshops at Le Rouvray, and is the European liaison for the European Quilt Expo, working for Quilts, Inc. in Houston.

Her creations have been juried into major international shows and published in magazines in the U.S., Japan, and New Zealand.

Besides being a teacher and a textile artist, she specializes in the history of the famous toile de Jouy.

She enjoys cooking and has a special interest in making people happy, whether in front of a quilt or around a table. When she is not touring the world, she lives outside Paris with her husband.

Cosabeth discovered the art of quiltmaking while living in California in the late 1970s. It quickly became her passion and vocation. After returning to France, she joined the team at Le Rouvray, where she worked and taught for twenty years.

A contemporary artist known for her work with color and transparency, her involvement in quilting has led her to teaching in France, throughout Europe, and in the U.S. Her quilts have appeared in art quilt expositions all over the world, and she has designed quilts for many prestigious French magazines.

The theme of Provence is very dear to Cosabeth's heart because of her family roots there. She spends most of her vacations at the family home in Provence, where she often cooks meals for the numerous members of her family.

She lives near Paris with her husband and their two young boys.

About the Authors

111

INDEX

C&T BOOK LIST

250 Continuous-Line Quilting Designs for Hand, Machine & Long-Arm Quilters, Laura Lee Fritz

Along the Garden Path: More Quilters and Their Gardens, Jean Wells & Valori Wells

Art of Classic Quiltmaking, The, Harriet Hargrave & Sharyn Craig

Block Magic: Over 50 Fun & Easy Blocks from Squares and Rectangles, Nancy Johnson-Srebro

Bouquet of Quilts, A: Garden-Inspired Projects for the Home, Jennifer Rounds & Cyndy Lyle Rymer

Butterflies & Blooms: Designs for Appliqué & Quilting, Carol Armstrong

Color Play: Easy Steps to Imaginative Color in Quilts, Joen Wolfrom

Come Listen to My Quilts: •Playful Projects •Mix & Match Designs, Kristina Becker

Cotton Candy Quilts: Using Feed Sacks, Vintage, and Reproduction Fabrics, Mary Mashuta

Do-It-Yourself Framed Quilts: Fast, Fun & Easy Projects, Gai Perry

Enchanted Views: Quilts Inspired by Wrought-Iron Designs, Dilys Fronks

Endless Possibilities: Using No-Fail Methods, Nancy Johnson-Srebro

Everything Flowers: Quilts from the Garden, Jean Wells & Valori Wells

Fabric Stamping Handbook, The: •Fun Projects •Tips & Tricks •Unlimited Possibilities, Jean Ray Laury

Fantastic Fabric Folding: Innovative Quilting Projects, Rebecca Wat

Flower Pounding: Quilt Projects for All Ages, Ann Frischkorn & Amy Sandrin

Freddy's House: Brilliant Color in Quilts, Freddy Moran

Garden-Inspired Quilts: Design Journals for 12 Quilt Projects, Jean Wells & Valori Wells

Heirloom Machine Quilting, Third Edition: Comprehensive Guide to Hand-Quilting Effects Using Your Sewing Machine, Harriet Hargrave

Imagery on Fabric, Second Edition: A Complete Surface Design Handbook, Jean Ray Laury

In the Nursery: Creative Quilts and Designer Touches, Jennifer Sampou & Carolyn Schmitz

Laurel Burch Quilts: Kindred Creatures, Laurel Burch

Lone Star Quilts and Beyond: Step-by-Step Projects and Inspiration, Jan Krentz

Make Any Block Any Size: Easy Drawing Method, Unlimited Pattern Possibilities, Sensational Quilt Designs, Joen Wolfrom

Mastering Quilt Marking: Marking Tools and Techniques, Choosing Stencils, Matching Borders and Corners, Pepper Cory

Paper Piecing Picnic: Fun-Filled Projects for Every Quilter, QNM

Paper Piecing with Alex Anderson: •Tips •Techniques •6 Projects, Alex Anderson

Photo Transfer Handbook, The: Snap It, Print It, Stitch It!, Jean Ray Laury

Quick Quilts for the Holidays: 11 Projects to Stamp, Stencil, and Sew, Trice Boerens

Quilted Garden, The: Design & Make Nature-Inspired Quilts, Jane Sassaman

Quilting Back to Front: Fun & Easy No-Mark Techniques, Larraine Scouler

Quilting With Carol Armstrong: •30 Quilting Patterns •Appliqué Designs •16 Projects, Carol Armstrong

Quilts from Europe, Gül Laporte

Show Me How to Machine Quilt: A Fun, No-Mark Approach, Kathy Sandbach

Strips 'n Curves: A New Spin on Strip Piecing, Louisa L. Smith

Through the Garden Gate: Quilters and Their Gardens, Jean Wells & Valori Well

---

**For more information
ask for a free catalog:**
C&T Publishing, Inc.
P.O. Box 1456
Lafayette, CA 94549
(800) 284-1114
Email: ctinfo@ctpub.com
Website: www.ctpub.com

For quilting supplies:
Cotton Patch Mail Order
3405 Hall Lane, Dept. CTB
Lafayette, CA 94549
(800) 835-4418 • (925) 283-7883
Email: quiltusa@yahoo.com
Website: www.quiltusa.com

PLEASE NOTE:
Fabrics used in the quilts shown may not be currently available since fabric manufacturers keep most fabrics in print for only a short time.

Watercolor of a typical old Provençal house